Trailside
Make Your Own Adventure

KAYAKING

KAYAKING
WHITEWATER AND TOURING BASICS
BY
STEVEN M. KRAUZER

Introduction

by

John Viehman

Illustrations by Ron Hildebrand

A TRAILSIDE SERIES GUIDE

W. W. NORTON & COMPANY

NEW YORK   LONDON

Copyright © 1995 by New Media, Incorporated
All rights reserved
Printed in the United States of America

The text of this book is composed in Bodoni Book with the display set in Triplex
Page composition by Tina Christensen
Color separations and prepress by Bergman Graphics, Incorporated
Manufacturing by R. R. Donnelley & Sons
Illustrations by Ron Hildebrand

Book design by Bill Harvey

Library of Congress Cataloging-in-Publication Data

Krauzer, Steven M., 1948—
Kayaking: whitewater and touring basics
introduction by John Viehman.
p.   cm. — (A Trailside series guide)
A companion volume to the television series, Trailside.
Includes bibliographical references and index.
1. Kayaking. I. Title. II. Series.
GV783.K73   1995   797.1'224—dc20   95-5527

ISBN 0-393-31336-0

W. W. Norton & Company, Inc., 500 Fifth Avenue, New York, N. Y. 10110
W. W. Norton & Company Ltd., 10 Coptic Street, London WC1A 1PU

2 3 4 5 6 7 8 9 0

CONTENTS

INTRODUCTION

The year was 1981, and I was one of the organizers (and part of the kitchen detail) for North America's first official Sea Kayaking Symposium, in Damariscotta, Maine. It was a multi-day event filled with lectures, world-class kayakers, instruction, and lots of on-water boat demonstrations from manufacturers. The air crackled with excitement, and you could feel the enthusiasm as would-be kayakers swarmed around boats and speakers.

I had discovered touring kayaks a year earlier, and was helping launch the concept to a nation. But as author Steve Krauzer points out in the pages that follow, kayaks have been around a long, long time. Some historians argue that the kayak, not the canoe, is the quintessential Native American craft, certainly of the Far North. Yet, while everything from bicycles to hula hoops have caught our fancy, kayaking as an American pastime never caught on. I didn't understand why until that day in Maine.

Americans had been scared away from kayaking, pure and simple. Years of watching daredevil whitewater paddlers charge bow-first into frothing, churning waves the size of cars generated excitement, but also bred fear. Then there's the idea of squeezing half your body into an egg-shaped opening not much larger than your waistline, which brings out the claustrophobe in all of us. And look what happens when kayaks tip over. You're trapped!

There was a perception that kayaking was only whitewater kayaking and that it was exclusively for thrill-seekers; that all kayaks were short, narrow, and inherently unstable; that all cockpit openings were tiny and constricting. For some reason the more commodious, stable touring, or sea, kayak and the calm-water venues for which it was designed had escaped our attention. For some reason most of us were convinced that extreme whitewater kayaking was the only form of kayaking, and therefore that we'd have to have a death wish to take up the sport.

During the symposium back in 1981, it dawned on me that all this paranoia didn't make sense. Each year more people choke on peanut butter than die while kayaking. The sport had gotten off to a bad start, but the introduction of the touring kayak to an American audience would change all that. They were longer, wider, more stable, had more generous cockpit openings than their whitewater cousins, and many even had foot-controlled rudders for easy maneuvering. These were kayaks designed to let paddlers relax and take in the world around them, vessels perfectly designed to let their occupants enjoy a special kind of freedom. There were tandem kayaks, too, so the sport even featured a friendly social element.

These days, touring symposia take place in at least 15 different locations nationwide, and thousands of people discover the craft each year. The surge toward flat-water kayaking has brought things into perspective. There still are plenty of kayakers leaping tall waves in a single stroke, and more power to them. But increasingly people are recognizing that there's more to this simplest of craft than sheer adrenaline. For that matter, kayakers are recognizing that river kayaking doesn't have to mean running truly terrifying rapids. It can mean choosing a kayak over an open canoe to paddle on relatively tame rivers and streams.

This book gives you the full spectrum of kayaking. Author Steve Krauzer has made it an introductory guide to both whitewater and flat-water kayaking. Now at first, you might find yourself a bit confused and overwhelmed by all the equipment and paddling techniques, as well as the knowledge you have to acquire about things like navigation and weather. But don't let that stop you. The beauty of kayaking is that you can come into the sport at any level and proceed at your own pace.

Now, let's go kayaking!

— *John Viehman*

THE WORLD
OF KAYAKING

Kayakers wax rhapsodic about their sport — the independence, the tranquility (or excitement), the spectacular scenery, and on and on. But here's the truth: One of the things they like best is that kayaking looks hard.

Watch the expressions of landlubbers when a kayaker slides smoothly through the surf to the beach, or high-braces into an eddy, pivoting smartly. There she executes an Eskimo roll, deliberately capsizing and then popping back up like a rubber bathtub duck. "Just practicing," she tells her companion, but both know she was out to impress the onlookers. From their expressions, she did; *must've taken a lot of work and a long time to learn to do that,* they are thinking.

Don't ruin it for them by letting the cat out of the bag: If you have never set butt to boat in your life, you are only a few hours of lessons from your first cruise. You'll find the frustration factor is low, and if you are of average physical condition with average large-motor-skill coordination, you'll quickly have many basic strokes down — and yes, that *does* include the Eskimo roll.

Although the natives of arctic North America have been building and piloting kayaks for centuries (see Chapter 6), as a sport kayaking is a relative youngster. It dates to 1905, when a German architectural student

The touring kayak (above) is a sleek, fast craft of ancient origins among the Aleut peoples, for whom it provided transportation and a platform from which to hunt. The whitewater kayak (opposite) is a modern adaptation of its flatwater cousin and is designed purely for the thrill of running rapids.

named Alfred Heurich built a folding kayak with a frame of bamboo and a sailcloth hull. Heurich may well get the nod as the first river rat; in that same year, he paddled the Isar River, near Munich.

But it was left to Johann Klepper, a tailor in nearby Rosenheim, to popularize kayaking. In 1907, after working with Heurich to perfect hull materials,

SCHOOL DAYS

Aside from the many excellent in-residence kayaking schools around the country (see Sources & Resources at the back of this book), look for "outpatient" treatment — short courses — in your area. Try YMCAs and similar athletic-oriented organizations, or the recreation department of a university. Larger retailers may also offer lessons, and can put you in touch with your local kayaking club.

The typical course meets in a swimming pool, or, in warmer climes, on a lake or pond. Cost and time investment tend to be reasonable. A couple of sessions will have you paddling with confidence, and with another couple of lessons you'll add your roll (the ability to right your kayak should it capsize). If the course is in-season, it might include, as "graduation," a guided shakedown trip on river or flatwater. "Loaner" equipment is usually provided.

Once you have minimal competency, don't overlook "open-kayak" nights; public and college swimming facilities are often made available for regular kayak practice sessions.

Klepper licensed Heurich's patent and began to produce kayaks for retail sale. The company that Klepper founded continues to market an extensive line of well-regarded folding boats to this day.

Over the next few decades, kayaks were best known as an adventurer's facturers in Germany, and dozens in other countries. Fold-boat expert Ralph Díaz believes that between the two world wars, the number of touring kayakers was even greater than it is today.

The rigid kayak appeared in the mid-1950s and began a march to

Sea kayaking doesn't have to be placid; surfing — riding breakers in a whitewater-style boat — is nearly as thrilling as running a river without the hazards of rocks and waterfalls.

craft. Kayaks crossed the English Channel, were paddled from Germany to India, and were carried by Roald Amundsen on his North Pole expedition of 1926, and by Admiral Richard Byrd on his South Pole expedition two years later.

The publicity generated by these daring endeavors drew enough common folk to the sport that by the 1930s there were at least eighty commercial manu-

market dominance. The first models were of fiberglass, but by the early 1980s kayaks of rotationally molded polyethylene plastic came to the fore. These extremely durable boats allowed the willing recreationalist to push kayaking into new realms, from towering ocean waves to steep thrashing whitewater rivers, and beyond.

Kayaking was introduced as an Olympic sport in 1936, and by 1992, there were ten kayak and canoe events (an Olympic-class "canoe" is a decked boat that looks and handles much like a kayak). Of the six events for men and four for women, the gold medal went to members of the German team in six of the competitions. However, the United States is starting to come into its own; in Double Canoe Slalom, Scott Strausbaugh and Joe Jacobi threaded the gates flawlessly to score gold for the United States Canoe and Kayak Team.

Whitewater kayaking can be as challenging or as easy-going as you choose. It is always a group sport, in which camaraderie and looking out for fellow boaters is highly valued.

You needn't aspire to either an intercontinental voyage or an Olympic medal to enjoy the pleasure of the double-bladed paddle. Kayaking is an eminently accessible sport that lends itself to every level of ambition, ability, and yen for pure fun.

Kayaking is a family sport. Aleut boys underwent a rite of passage when their kayaking instruction began at the age of twelve, but you need not even wait that long with your own kids. Indeed, for a humbling experience, lend your kayak to an eight-year-old. Unencumbered by the apprehensions and preconceptions you brought to your first voyage, the kid is likely to

In all water sports, safety must be taken seriously. Whitewater kayakers never take to the river without first donning life jacket and helmet.

DID YOU KNOW

Two pieces of evidence suggest that the kayak was invented as early as 7000 B.C. First, the islands reached by the Aleuts after crossing the Bering Strait are surrounded by rough seas featuring strong currents and year-round open leads. Some sort of kayak-like boat would have been necessary for settlement.

Second, datable skeletons of natives found in Aleut burial caves have huge arm bones compared to other remains of the same period. Unless they were pumping primitive iron, this supports the hypothesis that they were paddling solo boats.

handle the craft with enviable dexterity — and to enjoy it so much you'll have trouble getting your boat back.

While the initial cost of equipment is not inexpensive, once you plunk down your cash, that covers it. No lift tickets or greens fees are required.

Kayaking is a most aesthetically pleasing way to see water and country — and sometimes the only way. If you choose to become expert, you'll have access to waterways too roiling for an open canoe or even a raft.

But the most welcoming aspect of kayaking is that it allows you — encourages you, in fact — to choose your degree of skill and challenge. You can be perfectly satisfied with a lifetime of serene paddling in a placid

The sea kayaker's dream, a pristine, private inlet. This one is along the south side of Bligh Island, off the west coast of Vancouver Island, British Columbia, Canada, a Mecca for kayakers.

Sunrise along the Maine Island Trail, one of several coastal routes established in recent years for the ever-swelling ranks of sea kayak enthusiasts.

ocean lagoon, or you may one day challenge high waterfalls. Kayaking accepts any level of ambition, even among boaters on the same water. While your mate is popping "enders" in a ferocious hole, you might decide to sit it out in a comfortable eddy. Neither your friend nor the river minds.

TOOLS OF THE TRADE

A s the spectrum of kayaking activities is broad, so is the variety of craft. At one end is the long, fast, stable kayak dedicated to touring on flatwater; at the other extreme is the "squirt boat," a mere slip of a vessel that responds to even a whisper of current, and is meant to perform near-acrobatics on whitewater.

In this book, we're mainly concerned with the two "mainstream" classes of kayak from which most boaters choose. The touring kayak is often referred to as a sea kayak, but this is a misnomer. Thousands of "sea" kayaks never touch hull to salt water, and are used instead on lakes and other flatwater inland venues.

The second type is the white-water kayak, also known as a "slalom" kayak. Again, a misnomer: While originally designed in the 1970s to negotiate hanging "gates" in formal slalom competitions similar to those in Alpine skiing, river-runners have embraced the form for general sport where maneuverability and superb responsiveness are a boon.

Even "whitewater kayak" is a somewhat misleading term. The water need not be white (rapids intensive); the whitewater kayak is simply a superbly nimble, seaworthy craft for tackling moving water-courses of any velocity from the gentle to the mildly challenging to the thermonuclear.

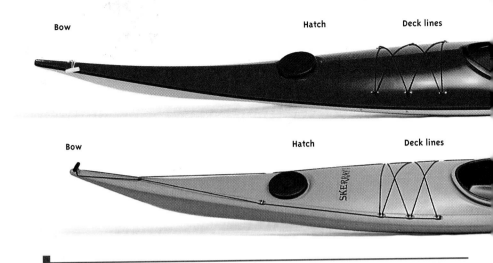

Bow   Hatch   Deck lines

Bow   Hatch   Deck lines

G E A R   T A L K

TWO TOURING KAYAKS

All kayaks are essentially the same: A narrow hull — not much wider than a human's hips — is entirely closed over with decking, except for a cockpit to allow the paddler entrance. Yet specialization makes some kayaks suited to cruising ocean waters, others to rushing down mountain streams. Here are two West-Greenland-style touring kayaks. They are long and sleek compared to their stubbier whitewater cousins (see pages 22 and 23), have relatively little rocker in their keel lines, and have water-tight compartments for gear stowage. The red kayak is fiberglass and features a rudder (flipped up here), while the blue kayak is rotomolded plastic and features a skeg (retracted here). Notice that the glass boat, while larger than the plastic one, is lighter. It is also nearly twice as costly, selling for around $2,000.

SPECIFICATIONS

MAKE Current Designs
MODEL Solstice ST (with rudder)
MATERIAL fiberglass
LENGTH 17 feet, 6 inches
WIDTH 24 inches
WEIGHT 50 pounds

MAKE Valley Canoe Products (U.K.,
  Great River Outfitter, importer)
MODEL Skerray RM
  (with retractable skeg)
MATERIAL rotationally molded poly-
  ethylene (rotomolded plastic)
LENGTH 17 feet
WIDTH 24 inches
WEIGHT 58 pounds

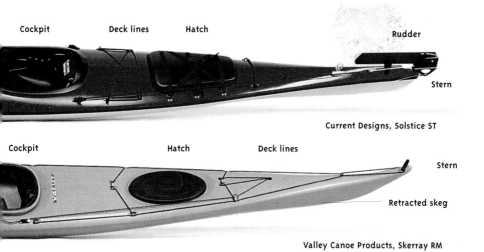

Cockpit   Deck lines   Hatch   Rudder   Stern

Current Designs, Solstice ST

Cockpit   Hatch   Deck lines   Stern   Retracted skeg

Valley Canoe Products, Skerray RM

KAYAK DESIGN 101: CHOOSING A BOAT

As you progress through your first lessons, the best course is not to choose a boat. Rent, borrow, swap with fellow students, and otherwise try as many types, brands, and shapes of kayaks as you can.

In time your preferences will develop, and to an extent they are subjective. You would not buy a backpack that digs into your kidneys, a mountain bike whose frame size threatens to drive your knees into your jaw, or hiking boots that fit as loosely as clown shoes. In the same way, depend on your instinct as to whether a particular boat simply "feels good"; indeed, the kayak you settle on definitely should feel right.

When you've become an intermediate and are ready to invest in a boat of your own, it's a help to understand the design considerations that affect a boat's purpose and performance.

It's easy to see that the distinguishing difference between a touring and whitewater kayak is size:

The larger a boat, the greater its stability — and the less maneuverability it will have. This trade-off is true of any watercraft. Think of an ocean liner. Now think of a surfboard.

Five design aspects make the major contributions to what a kayak will do, and how well.

Length

Length is obviously related to size. To choose a length for your touring kayak, see Chapter 6; for whitewater boats, see Chapter 10.

Rocker

A touring kayak's keel-line is nearly flat, whereas a whitewater boat's keel-line curves upward fore and aft so that the bow and stern are, on average, a half foot higher than the midpoint. The more pronounced this curve, the greater the boat's rocker.

Rocker affects the area of hull that contacts the water called the working waterline. Try standing flat-footed with

Stern

Cockpit

PROLINE perception

Bow

Cockpit

Pirouette S

feet apart. It's hard to fall over, but also hard to turn. Now bring your feet together and rise to tiptoes. You can pirouette like a ballet dancer, but get too vigorous about it and you're kissing the carpet.

Rocker works the same way. As the working waterline is reduced, the boat's ability to "spin on a dime" increases — and this applies whether you wish to spin or the water wishes to spin you. A whitewater kayak is designed for quick maneuverability and so has lots of

rocker. A touring kayak is designed for greater stability and straight-line speed and so has little rocker. Maneuverability and speed are incompatible; the more rocker in a boat's keel, the easier it will be to turn, but the slower it will be.

Flare & Chine

Flare refers to the hull's appearance in cross-section, and profoundly effects a boat's stability; the more flare from keel to the point where the sides meet the deck, the more resistant to cap-

sizing a boat will be. Chine refers to the point where the bottom of a boat turns upward to become its side (see

Flare

None

Moderate

Chine

Soft

Hard

Coaming

Bow

Perception Corsica Overflow

Coaming

Stern

Perception Pirouette S

GEAR TALK

TWO WHITEWATER KAYAKS

Whitewater kayaks like these two models are designed for maneuverability above all else. They are shorter and slower than their touring cousins (see pages 20 and 21), but they can turn on a dime as they make their way through rapids. Among whitewater boats, there is a high level of specialization, with some models, like the Overflow, suited to all-around river running by beginners and other models, like the Pirouette, specially designed for more advanced paddlers and sometimes called playboats in reference to the stunts they can perform in experienced hands.

SPECIFICATIONS

MAKE Perception
MODEL Corsica Overflow
MATERIAL rotationally molded polyethylene (rotomolded plastic)
LENGTH 10 feet
WIDTH 23³/4 inches
WEIGHT 39 pounds
VOLUME 77 gallons
PADDLER WEIGHT RANGE 100–200 pounds

MAKE Perception
MODEL Pirouette S
MATERIAL rotationally molded polyethylene (rotomolded plastic)
LENGTH 11 feet
WIDTH 23 inches
WEIGHT 39 pounds
VOLUME 62 gallons
PADDLER WEIGHT RANGE 100–200 pounds

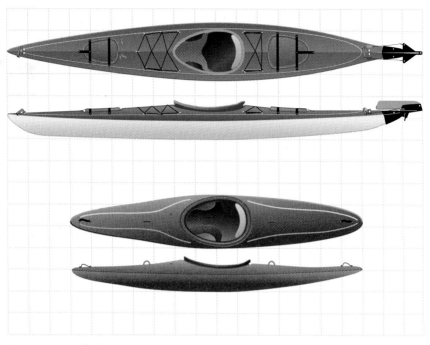

The touring kayak (top) has greater volume than the whitewater kayak (bottom) thanks to its greater length, but also because it is generally slightly wider and has a deeper draft. The keel line of the touring kayak is nearly flat, giving it greater straight line speed, while the keel line of the whitewater kayak has pronounced rocker, making it slower but far more maneuverable.

illustration). Most whitewater kayaks have little or no discernible chine.

Touring kayaks generally have more flare and a somewhat harder chine than their whitewater cousins, giving touring boats greater stability. The whitewater kayak's rounded hull makes it tippy, but also easier to roll upright if it *does* capsize, and extremely nimble.

Volume

As a ship's size is measured in tonnage, the overall size of a kayak is measured in volume, the quantity of water that will fill the empty boat to the brim. An average whitewater kayak has a volume in the neighborhood of 60 to 70 gallons; a typical touring kayak has a volume

around 100 gallons. Again, a bigger boat is easier to keep upright and more difficult to turn quickly.

Stability vs. Maneuverability

If you are wondering which of these two factors should most concern you in choosing a kayak, the answer is: It's not that important, especially as you embark on the sport.

You'd prefer a less equivocal answer. Okay. Choose a boat that is as maneuverable as possible given your other needs.

But, honest, it really *isn't* all that important. All non-radically designed kayaks — even an unwieldy-appearing

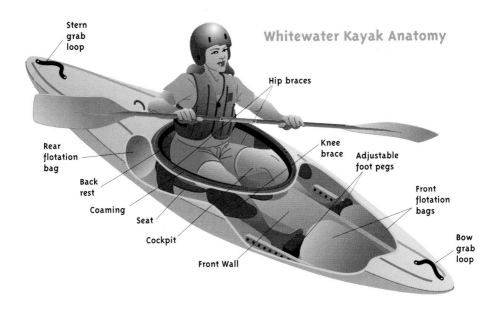

Stern grab loop

Hip braces

Rear flotation bag

Back rest

Coaming

Seat

Cockpit

Knee brace

Adjustable foot pegs

Front flotation bags

Bow grab loop

Front Wall

22-foot tandem (two-person) touring boat — have good to excellent *directional stability*, a term referring to the boat's tendency to maintain a straight course. The more pronounced rocker of the whitewater kayak does make it more likely to act as if it has a mind of its own about which way to go, but as soon as you have a few paddle strokes under your hat, keeping it in a straight line comes easily.

Initial stability is a given kayak's tendency to remain upright at rest, and in both standard tourers and whitewater boats it is much greater than the slim, needle-nosed shape suggests. With a paddler in place, his bottom a few inches from the hull, the center of gravity is very low, at about belt-buckle level. Preconceptions about tippiness will evaporate within minutes of your first entry into a boat. Keep this secret from landlubbers,

too. Let them believe that kayaks are as tippy as twigs — it adds to the mystique.

For now, forget about tippiness and concentrate on acquiring some basic techniques. You'll learn to kayak in warm water and under controlled conditions, and every skill you'll develop in the basic lessons is common to any kayak in any sort of water. Elementary technique is just that: elemental to the sport no matter how far you intend to take it. If you've made a tentative decision as to whether you'll be touring or running rivers, there's no reason not to learn in the appropriate boat if it is available. If not, don't be concerned. No matter what your training craft, all of your beginning lessons will stand you in good stead when you hit the water.

And soon you will — but first, a trip to the haberdasher.

THE WELL-DRESSED KAYAKER: HOW TO FIT IN

Unlike a canoeist or rafter, a kayaker does not sit in the boat — he *wears* it. When a kayaker moves, so does his kayak.

Like any "garment," when you try on a kayak you're looking for fit and comfort. Five points of contact are relevant: feet, knees, butt, back, and hips.

Feet are set against a brace, usually a pair of pedals but occasionally a flat platform, that adjusts for kayakers of different heights. Braces accommodate the knees, and should be padded; if padding is not part of the original equipment, low-density foam is available from outfitters and can be glued or taped in place. If the seat, backrest, and foam hip pads are right for you, and hold your lower body snugly but not confiningly, you've found a kayak that suits your shape.

But double-check: Can you flex your ankles and knees to take some pressure off the foot pegs, so that your leg muscles can relax in flatwater? Yet if you cock your ankles at an angle of about 30 degrees, do you feel snugly locked in?

If so, you are solidly "in costume," and at the same time unconfined. Now that you know how it should fit, it is time to consider the "fabrics" for your suit.

Kayak Materials

With the exception of the folding touring kayak (see Chapter 6), most contemporary kayaks are made of either fiberglass or some type of poly-ethylene plastic. Manufacturers also offer combinations; one of the more common is a Kevlar/fiberglass hybrid.

Each of the three hull materials has both advantages and disadvantages — some objective, others vigorously argued by proponents of one material over another. Let's consider the upsides and downsides by the former criterion, and leave the subjective considerations to campsite debate.

The principal issues are cost, weight, and durability. When all are considered, it is safe to recommend rotationally molded plastic as the best choice for a first kayak.

Rotationally Molded Plastic

Polyethylene kayaks are virtually indestructible. Drag a rotomold boat over a thousand rocky beaches and ding hundreds of river rocks, and the only evidence will be inconsequential surface scratches. They are also the least expensive, and are produced in the widest variety of models and lengths.

Weight gain is the greatest disadvantage; a rotomold boat will tip the scales at about 10 percent more poundage than fiberglass. This is significant if you anticipate a lot of portaging, but insignificant when the boat is afloat.

Fiberglass

Fiberglass boats are typically 10 percent lighter than rotomolds, and you can expect to pay about 20 percent more for this advantage (see "The Price List" in this chapter). Fiberglass also demands more care, both in repairing of rips and in hosing off and storage after saltwater exposure. Still, unless you plan to take on large rocks at high speeds, fiberglass boats are satisfactorily durable.

Kevlar

A typical 19-foot touring kayak that tips the scale at 66 pounds in fiberglass will weigh only 45 pounds in Kevlar. Along with its light weight, Kevlar is extremely strong (you probably are most familiar with it as the material of bulletproof vests). The tariff for these advantages is significant: A Kevlar kayak can cost twice as much as the same model in rotomold.

THE REST OF THE ENSEMBLE

Besides the boat itself, there are five items without which no kayaker leaves home: paddle, spray skirt, flotation, personal flotation device (PFD), and appropriate garb.

The Paddle

Since its earliest days in the hands of native kayakers of far-northern America, the kayak paddle, already a cunning piece of equipment, has continued to evolve. Its twin blades obviate the need for the crossover maneuver a canoeist must employ, and the first time a brisk late-afternoon breeze hits you in the face, you'll truly appreciate its "feathered" design.

"Feathering" means that the blades are offset at an angle between 70 and 90 degrees. The result is that as you draw a stroke with one blade, the other is edge-on to the wind, cut-

CRUNCH TIME

One other difference between fiberglass and rotomold should be borne in mind if you aspire to run *major* whitewater. A large volume of fast-moving river that pins a boat against a rock or other obstruction has the power to bend it in half (for more on "broaching," see Chapter 13). In this dangerous situation, a fiberglass kayak should tear; a rotomolded boat will not, and can trap the boater inside.

To help protect against this eventuality, rotomolded boats have a two-part rigid foam center brace, a vertically mounted reinforcing spacer between hull and deck. One segment runs from behind the backstrap to the stern, the other between the boater's legs to the bow. The braces provide increased rigidity and protection in cases of casual bow or stern contact with rocks. The cockpit, however, remains the weak link. Should you broach in water powerful enough to fold your boat, it will fold at this midpoint — not a good thing, given that this is exactly where you are sitting.

Basic Paddle Styles

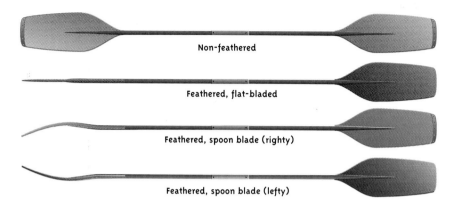

Non-feathered

Feathered, flat-bladed

Feathered, spoon blade (righty)

Feathered, spoon blade (lefty)

ting smoothly through it rather than acting as an annoying mini-sail bent on blowing you off-course.

The considerations in choosing a paddle are material and blade shape. Most paddles are fashioned of either laminated hardwood such as ash or a hollow aluminum shaft with plastic blades. Weight is about the same; the principal difference is aesthetic. Without question, a wooden paddle is a more beautiful object, and it is more often the choice of committed kayakers, some of whom argue that wood makes for a more flexible, forgiving paddle.

Ask twelve kayakers how to gauge paddle length, and you are likely to get thirteen answers. In general, touring paddles are longer than whitewater paddles, and their blades are somewhat smaller. What length fits you depends on the size kayak you paddle, your strength, and the conditions in which you plan to paddle. Finding the right size paddle is partly a matter of

trying out various lengths to learn what is most comfortable and consulting with an experienced outfitter or instructor.

Here is one general rule of thumb I would follow: It is better to err on the side of a shorter paddle than to be stuck with one that is too long. In general, using an excessively long paddle makes for an inefficient stroke.

The paddle's blades are either flat or "spooned." A spooned blade's power face (the side that addresses the water, the inside of the "spoon") takes a somewhat more powerful bite of the water, as long as surface area is equal — but surface area *isn't* necessarily equal. Either shape will serve to propel you forward, but the novice learning the roll usually finds the flat blade to be both psychologically and practically more supportive.

Two-part paddles that connect through a ferrule are available. Some wobble can develop with use, but if you go with a reputable manufacturer

Kayaking's double-bladed paddles come in many shapes and sizes. 1) A basic, flat-bladed paddle with polypropylene blade and aluminum shaft suited to touring and whitewater. 2) Straightforward whitewater paddle with slightly spooned, plastic blade and vinyl-covered aluminum shaft. 3) Top-of-the-line wooden touring paddle. 4) A high-end, lightweight touring paddle with slightly spooned, fiberglass blade and fiberglass shaft. 5) Another high-end fiberglass touring paddle with narrower blade. 6) "Wing" paddle designed for flatwater racing and touring, it has such a radical blade that it requires a slightly modified paddling technique.

and find a trustworthy outfitter, this is unlikely. Two-parters are excellent for the spare paddle you should consider strapping under your rear deck lines when crossing large expanses of open water. Another benefit is that they can be configured for the lefty, the righty, and the maverick who prefers less than standard feathering or, as is not uncommon among tourers, none at all.

The Spray Skirt

If, in wearing the kayak, the boat is your "britches," then the spray skirt is your "belt." It helps keep you in and the water out.

The skirt makes you and your kayak watertight, whether you are splashing through deck-washing waves or are upside down and about to execute a near-effortless Eskimo roll (and you will — trust me on this). It consists of two parts: the tunnel, which is what fits snugly around your waist; and the skirt itself, which snaps over the rim of the boat's cockpit, called the coaming.

Water-resistant (treated) nylon with a shock cord sewn into its hem is the norm for touring models, while it has largely been replaced by neoprene

The nylon spray skirt (middle) is especially suited to warm weather paddling in touring kayaks. This skirt, like many touring models, features an accessory pocket. Taut, warm, durable, neoprene skirts (top and bottom) are required for whitewater kayaking. The spray skirt must be precisely fitted to the kayak.

(a synthetic rubber) as the material of choice for whitewater boats. Skirts are fit to the boat, so make sure yours is designed for the kayak you plan to use it with. Don't forget to try it on both yourself and the boat; it has to fit your girth as well as the boat's.

Flotation

Unlike a canoe, a swamped kayak is more dense than the water, and will sink like a stone. Although in most instances of capsizing a kayak will trap air inside, why take the chance?

In touring kayaks, flotation is usu-

GEAR TALK

WATER WEIGHT

Any amount of water inside can make a kayak unwieldy. A gallon of water weighs about $8\frac{1}{3}$ pounds; if you have left your boat after capsizing and must swim the boat to shore, you're wrestling with a beast that outweighs you by about two to one. With air bags in place, you'll be pulling a lot less water weight, and emptying the kayak will be far easier.

ally built in, in the form of airtight bulkheads fore and aft of the cockpit, which do double duty as cargo space. Whitewater kayaks, however, rarely carry gear, since the extra weight compromises maneuverability in the more challenging river situations these boats tackle. Instead of bulkheads, they depend on air bags, single or, more commonly, dual, since the interior of nearly all new whitewater boats is divided by a reinforcing brace; the dual bags fit on either side of the vertical brace. Air bags are easily inflated with lung power, through blow tubes, which are tucked out of the way after inflation.

PFDs

Remember that orange "horse-collar" life jacket you wore while learning to swim at summer camp? Forget it.

Personal flotation devices (PFDs) are approved and categorized by the U.S. Coast Guard. The horse collar falls into Type II; what you want is a Type III. It's a sleeveless nylon-sheathed package of closed-density foam slats that zips up the front and is additionally secured by a waist tie. Pick a Type III that is kayak specific, either ending around belly-button level or with extended flares that fold up upon the vest's body to avoid jamming against the spray skirt's deck. The latter is slightly more constricting, but more buoyant and versatile, since you can fold down the flares for greater

GEAR TALK

AIR RAID

Never store a kayak with the air bags fully inflated, because temperature increases can cause them to expand and burst. On especially hot days, it's a good idea to let out some air when stopping for lunch; it's a prudent precaution, and a few puffs will bring them back to taut.

PFDs (personal flotation devices) are required gear for all safety-conscious boaters, but particularly whitewater kayakers. Many styles are available, including 1) an all-purpose, zip-front, short-waist model; 2) a pullover vest popular among racers; 3) a short-waisted vest, with chest pocket and sleeves for flares, designed for tourers; and 4) a zip-front model with knife loop, mesh pocket, and waist-tie.

comfort when using the same vest for canoeing or rafting.

Just as you automatically fasten your seat belt, always wear your PFD (and note that in waters under U.S. Coast Guard jurisdiction, it's required). Zip all zippers, snap all snaps, and fasten all belts; the right hydraulic can pull an unsecured PFD over your head as easily as you'd strip off your T-shirt.

WHAT TO WEAR WHILE YOU'RE WEARING THE BOAT

The clothing equation is, frankly, not completely solvable. The problem is that air temperature and water temperature can routinely vary by 40 degrees. Take a brilliantly sunny spring day in the northern Rockies. It may be bathing-suit weather on the beach, but only a few hours earlier the river was mountainside snow, and its voyage downstream has hardly given it a chance to warm appreciably.

Begin with a realistic evaluation of how much time you plan to spend above water, and how much time in it. If you're hitting flatwater with no intention of rolling, you'll be comfortable and safe in the clothing you'd wear for a brisk stroll. But if you plan to do a lot of playing in serious rapids, you'll expect to be upside down frequently, and those brisk baths call for dress that keeps you toasty. Besides, if hard paddling down a long stretch of flatwater between rapids puts you in a lather, you can always execute a quick roll for a cool down.

The Drysuit

The drysuit is at the warm-and-cozy extreme of the clothing line. A loose-fitting, head-to-foot insulated and rubberized garment designed to keep water out completely, it will keep you comfortable for extended periods even in arctic conditions (for the techies in the crowd, the freezing point of seawater is 28.6 degrees Fahrenheit), if you wear insulating layers beneath it.

Drysuits do have a number of disadvantages. They are expensive, somewhat constraining, and some older, one-piece designs present an unlikely but nonetheless sobering danger: If an accidental tear occurs while you are in the drink, these drysuits can fill with a volume of water great enough to overcome your PFD's flotation ability. And the rubber neck, wrist, and ankle gaskets are quite prone to tearing, and in any event must be replaced periodically as they wear out.

HUMAN ICE CUBES

Water, especially water that moves, is a more thermodynamically efficient medium than air. Because of its density, it stores energy in the form of heat well, and releases it slowly. Any time an object — an ice cube in a gin and tonic, or a human in an ocean — is either colder or warmer than the liquid medium, nature desires equilibrium. The human, for instance, will release heat, actually warming the water in the immediate vicinity — but in the end, the cold of the water will bring the human down to its level, because there is more of it than of you.

Even in water at a relatively balmy 65 degrees, immersion for a long enough period will bring your temperature to the same reading. This is not salubrious. In fact, it is fatal, and not only that, before morbidity sets in, you'll be darned uncomfortable.

For more on hypothermia and other temperature-related phenomena, see Chapter 13.

The Wetsuit

The wetsuit is a body-molded neoprene sheath that, when you hit the drink, traps water between your skin and the material. The water, when warmed by your body heat, provides a second layer of efficient insulation.

Wetsuit design runs the gamut from full neck-to-wrist-to-ankle coverage to vest tops and shorts. Your choice should be guided by both the conditions you expect to encounter and your personal response to cold. Various wetsuit components can also be combined; for example, during chill spring runoff you might wear a long-sleeved wetsuit pullover over a sleeveless "Farmer John" top, which, a month later when snowmelt ends, will be sufficient by itself.

From top left: The drysuit, warmest garment in the kayaker's wardrobe, is designed to keep all water away from the skin, but should only be used when conditions require, since it is somewhat constricting. The neoprene "farmer john" style wetsuit is a popular choice for warmth and comfort. Lycra/neoprene blends in T-shirts and shorts and all-neoprene material in gloves and booties provide warmth and comfort. Top right: A nose clip attached to a neck strap is worn by some whitewater kayakers.

Warm-Weather Attire

If you don't expect to spend time in cold water, the closet probably harbors all you'll need in the way of clothing. Eschew cotton, such as the T-shirt; cotton absorbs water rather than wicking it away from the skin. Apply the same "layering" principle you would for hiking or backpacking, making your choices from the synthetic or wool clothing groups. A long-sleeved polypropylene jersey is an excellent against-the-skin foundation that will warm you even if it is wet. For the second layer, a windbreaker or rain shell is fine, although a kayak-specific option is a paddling jacket, a loose-fitting pullover made of treated nylon or similar material. One designed with neoprene closures at neck and wrists that are fastened with Velcro does a fine job of keeping water out.

As you plan your wardrobe for the weather and water conditions, bear in mind that your PFD (which of course you will be wearing at all times) also

No whitewater kayaker should ever hit the water without a properly fitted helmet designed for the purpose. Helmets should provide full coverage of the forehead, temples, and ears and be securely strapped in place.

THE PRICE LIST

Kayaks and related equipment vary in cost, but you can expect that your expense in outfitting for the sport will be within 10 percent of the prices on this list.

TOURING KAYAKS

Single-seat rotomold	$550-$1,200
Single-seat fiberglass	$1,000-$2,200
Single-seat folding	$2,500-$3,000

For tandem (two-person) touring kayaks, add 40 percent

WHITEWATER KAYAKS

Rotomold	$650-$825
Kevlar	$900-$1,200

Paddles	
Wood	$200
Metal shaft/plastic blade	$100-$200
Spray skirt	$40-$90
Float bags, full set	$40
Helmet (whitewater)	$40
Type III PFD (life jacket)	$50-$75
Drysuit	$300
Wetsuit	
Farmer John	$120
Shorts	$60
Vests	$40
Gloves	$25
Neoprene booties	$40
Nose clips	$2.99
Don't forget your Metzgar	$3.99

Sport sandals are preferred footwear among many kayakers.

more heavy-duty boating consider "pogies" that strap around the paddle shaft. "Pogies" are harder to lose, usually warmer since they are akin to mittens, and allow you to "wear" the paddle much as you wear your boat.

provides a torso-warming layer.

Digits

Hand- and footgear serve both to keep extremities warm and to protect against other insults of the environment. Water-softened hands are prey to blisters, a real pain-in-the-palm. Stand-alone paddling gloves will do the trick in most situations, but for

In forgiving temperatures, river sandals or even an old pair of sneakers are fine. Neoprene booties, or "wet shoes," are your best bet for colder water, but choose the thickest sole available. Thin soles make for awkward and uncomfortable stumbling over rock shoals and other shoreline topology.

GEAR TALK

SECURITY ABOVE THE NECK

Herewith a handy and inexpensive piece of gear, involving kayaker Jim Metzgar.

First, consider Jim Metzgar, a fine kayaker who several years back became notorious among his western Montana boating mates. Not for his roll, which was sturdy; not for his enthusiasm, which was profound; nor for his strokes, which were elegant. Metzgar's claim to fame was that he lost three pairs of spectacles in one summer, until it occurred to him that a safety strap might just be a good investment. In recognition, the eyeglass strap was dubbed by his pals the "Metzgar."

Don't forget your Metzgar.

ONTO THE WATER

In *Hondo*, one of Louis L'Amour's most widely read Westerns, the eponymous hero teaches the widder-woman's son to swim. He uses a method that, depending on one's experience as a youth, appears either barbaric or effective.

Hondo tosses the tot into the drink and says, in effect, "Paddle, you little muskrat!"

Needless to say, the kid learns to swim — although when he comes up sputtering, he's hardly doing an Olympic-quality breaststroke. Arguably this doesn't matter: He's above water, he's conquered his apprehensions, he's moving forward, and he's prepared to learn more.

At least in fiction. In real life,

there is something to be said for both sides of the issue.

Kids are blessed. Put one in a kayak, deliver an elementary discourse on technique, suffer through the child's disdain at your didactic approach — and then watch while he pilots your boat with *savoir faire*. In a heartbeat he is steering with aplomb, crossing an eddy line or launching through surf, and instinctively executing strokes and braces.

But for those of us in our advanced years — over the age of eighteen, let's say — we'll forget Hondo's assertive sink-or-swim technique in favor of the methodological approach. Let's begin on dry land — your front lawn, for instance.

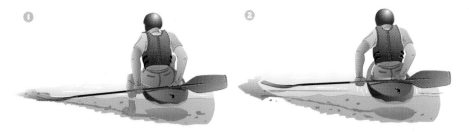

Boarding the Kayak. 1) With the kayak in ankle-deep water, place the end of the paddle shaft across the rear of the coaming, and hold it in place with your fingers inside the coaming and your thumb around the shaft. With the opposite hand, grip the shaft just beyond the boat's side. Now set one foot into the cockpit, and sit on the back deck, being careful not to put too much strain on the paddle. It's meant to provide balance, NOT support your weight. 2) Draw your other leg into the cockpit and slide yourself down onto the seat.

BOARDING THE KAYAK

Step into the spray skirt and pull up the tunnel to just below breast level, then roll the back inward so you won't end up sitting on it. Put on your PFD. That's all there is to preparation. You are ready to be piped aboard.

The one time when a kayak wants to be awkwardly tippy is on entering or exiting, since in the process the combination boat-boater center of gravity is high. To overcome this, use your paddle as a steadying outrigger.

If you are boarding in calm shallows, you can safely set the paddle in the water while securing the spray

The Control and Slip Hands. 1) As you complete the power stroke on the control side (in this case the right side, since the kayaker is right handed), begin to rotate your body toward the slip side. 2) Bend your control hand at the wrist and let the paddle shaft slip in a loosened grip from your slip hand into the proper paddle-blade position for 3) the power stroke on the slip side. For the next control-side stroke, flex the right wrist to its original position, returning the paddle blade to its original position.

skirt; otherwise, balance it across the front deck.

The hassle-free way to get most spray skirts in place is to begin by threading the hem around the rear arc of the coaming. Hook the front over the forward point, and finish up by snapping the sides into place.

Now you are snugly at one with the boat — and quite possibly thinking that in the event of a capsize, you'd like to be not at one with the boat as quickly as possible. Pull the grab loop at the head end of the skirt away from you and up. If the skirt fits the boat correctly, a moderate effort will free it from the tip. Now pull toward you and the sides and back will release. Boost yourself up from the seat, and you'll be pleasantly reassured of your complete freedom.

HOLDING THE PADDLE

The paddle blades' feathered configuration dictates that to present the

---

GEAR TALK

TALE OF THE TELLTALE

You may wish to choose a paddle with a shaft that is oval in cross section. This provides a "telltale" that acts as a tactile reminder of the control hand's correct position.

If your paddle is round-shafted you can add a telltale yourself, by using duct or marine tape to affix one 6-inch length of $1/8$-inch-wide dowel at each of the two grip points. Situate each dowel so that it is under the middle set of knuckles of either hand when that hand is in the correct position to power its stroke.

Control-side Stroke   Slip-side Stroke

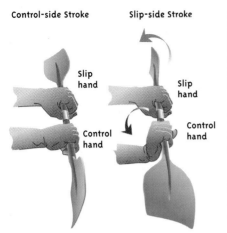

Slip
hand

Slip
hand

Control
hand

Control
hand

Gripping the Paddle. The control hand's grip never changes during paddling, but the control hand's wrist flexes. The slip hand loosens between strokes to allow the shaft to rotate back and forth through a quarter turn.

Below: A right-handed whitewater kayaker on the verge of making a slip-side power stroke. Note the flex in the right wrist to put the left paddle blade in the correct position to address the water with its power face. Opposite: The control hand in position as the stroke is begun. Notice how the paddler is centered over his boat.

power face to the water, adjustment is necessary depending on which side of the boat you are stroking.

Each of your hands has a different job to do in making this adjustment. Assuming that you are a righty, that will be your "control hand."

Grip the shaft about a fist width in from the top of the right blade. With the wrist unbent, that blade should be in position to address the water.

Through two strokes (first on the right side, then the left), the control hand's grip does not change.

Now grasp the shaft with the other (or "slip") hand at the same distance from the opposite blade and at a natural angle, and mime the two strokes.

HITTING THE WATER

For safety, you'll never kayak alone until you

A touring kayaker, making an efficient power stroke, sends his sleek craft speeding forward. Note how his left arm is pushing the paddle shaft forward as his right arm pulls it back for maximum power.

are a seasoned kayaker. On your first time afloat, a buddy is especially valuable for lending a helping hand.

Begin by setting your boat in enough water to float it. Fight the urge to have your pal hold it steady while you enter; instead, use the paddle-outrigger technique to climb aboard.

Paddle out into calm water that is about waist deep. Some guidance from your chum to get where you want to be is acceptable at this stage.

For safety's sake, beginners should not kayak alone; whitewater kayakers should never paddle challenging water solo.

Before continuing, consider the efficiency of the kayak/kayaker engine. No matter the design of your boat, you are "drafting" little water compared to a canoe or raft, a boon when it comes to resistance against forward motion. The boat's streamline and low center of gravity further favor movement. Feel how the weight distribution of boat and boater works to keep you upright.

To move this sleek craft requires no more than average upper-body strength, unless you intend to race (see Chapter 14 for racing and other competitive kayaking sports). Without any current or a headwind, you can easily propel the boat at a sustained speed of 3 miles an hour with

Not only the arm muscles, but also those of the torso contribute to the energy-efficient propulsion of the kayak.

only minimal demands on arms and shoulders.

You'll quickly learn that the joints and muscles of the hips and abdominal

The comfortable, efficient way for two kayakers to carry their boats and gear to the water's edge.

region are much more key. That's nice, because this happens to be the strongest mechanical system in most human bodies. In a standing position, if you bend at the waist and rise erect again you will have lifted perhaps 80 pounds — your entire body from the pelvis up — without effort or exertion. Unless you've been spending a heck of a lot of time down at the health club, you'd be hard pressed to muscle up such a weight using only arms and upper body.

Experiment to see how handy that hip system will soon become. Keeping the upper body perpendicular to the surface, rock the boat to one side by cocking your waist, then bring the boat level again by snapping your hips back to normal position.

Before long, you should be able to dip the boat 45 degrees to the side — then flick it level with almost no effort. The "wearing-the-boat" metaphor becomes more clear, and your confidence in the kayak's initial stability is reaffirmed.

In fact, all the moves you've made so far in the boat, on land and water, from boarding to rudimentary paddling to rocking, point to one conclusion. It may seem counterintuitive, but intellectually it's undeniable: A kayak does not tip easily. Even if you're still not entirely ready to buy this proposition whole-hog, will you take an option on it?

Good — because it's time to tip it over.

The notion of hanging upside down underwater in a boat to which you are attached is disconcerting. Before long, it won't have to be — it will merely be a passing phase on the way to the Eskimo roll that brings you up. But even after you've got your roll down, there will come rare occasions when it can fail you, and while you are perfecting it, you will surely take a swim or three.

THE WET EXIT

Bailing out from a capsize is a maneuver to be practiced before you have to deal with its involuntary version. It's the quickest way to convince yourself that capsizing is not to be feared. Actually, it's a piece of cake.

You've already learned how easily you can release your spray skirt. This part of your outfit is your new best friend, fitting tightly enough to make you feel secure, yet easily unhooked when you want out.

Now, set aside this book and hold your breath for 30 seconds.

You are barely winded. The wet exit will take a third of that time.

Back in waist-deep water (make

EMPTYING A SWAMPED BOAT

After you've bailed out from a capsize and pulled your boat to shore, you'll have to do something about that boatful of water. You can empty it alone, or with your buddy.

❶ With a friend assisting, pick up the kayak by the grab loops and seesaw it until most of the water has flowed out. The remainder can be pumped or sponged out.

❷ Elevate the bow or stern somewhat so that you can achieve the same seesawing motion to drain the water through the cockpit.

Assisted

Unassisted

sure there are no obstacles below the surface), with your friend standing by for company and reassurance, hold onto your paddle and throw your upper body to the side to make the boat turn turtle.

Shimmy your control hand to the middle of the paddle shaft (the paddle should be parallel to the boat), and then slowly count to three. Pass the seconds conceptualizing the moves you are about to make.

With your slip hand, reach forward and pull the grab loop forward and then down to free the skirt as you did on dry land. Set the paddle parallel against the side of the boat and, without letting the paddle go, also grip the coaming on either side of the cockpit. Somersault out, taking the paddle with you. A second later, your PFD bobs you to the surface.

Before heading for shore, don't forget to take your capsized boat with you. Spin it around so you can take hold of either the bow or stern grab loop, and pull it back to shore.

That's all there is to it.

Now that we know how to exit from an upside-down kayak, let's talk about keeping the boat right side up.

There's more than one way to carry a boat, as this kayaker demonstrates. His forehead is protected by the seat's back rest.

THE
ESKIMO
ROLL

Remember that grammar-school lesson on the airfoil which was supposed to show you why a plane can fly — and remember your reaction? It probably went something like this: Three hundred tons of Boeing 747 is supposed to stay in the sky because of *unequal air pressure*? Yeah, right.

So instead of a similarly tedious explanation of why all of your paddle moves in a kayak depend on the fact that hydrodynamics are capable of keeping you upright in the most extreme situations, forget science in favor of a demonstration.

Wade into the water up to your navel. Form a stiff, closed-fingered palm and press down on the surface.

There's resistance — no surprise.

Now sweep your hand across the surface and, as you do, press again. There's a lot more resistance.

You've just executed your first brace.

BRACING

Every time your paddle is in contact with water, whether the blade is parallel to the water's surface, as in the brace, or pulling through the water in a stroke, you are supporting yourself on a hydrofoil. However, hark back to that 747: Sitting static on the runway, it is unlikely to spontaneously levitate.

To provide support your paddle must be moving relative to the water.

Above: Children take to kayaks like ducks to water. Here is a first lesson in the low brace. Opposite: A low brace. Note the position of the arms: low and close to the body.

If the boat is coursing forward, the water can do enough moving to fill the bill. If the boat is still, you must provide the dynamics by moving the paddle; by performing a brace.

THE LOW BRACE

To translate your hand brace into a paddle move, extend the control-hand blade and place it flat against the water's surface, with the backside of the power face on the water. Your right arm should be slightly bent, your left elbow against the ribs. With a smooth motion, sweep the blade back and forth at a cadence of about 2 seconds per

sweep, pressing down gently.

Now lean toward the blade, using your hips to tilt the boat toward what would appear to be capsize. Instead — *mirabile dictu* — the hydrofoil that your blade has become provides a support of reassuring strength. You've done a low, or sculling, brace.

Practicing the low brace in still water, "push the envelope" of how far to the side you can tilt the boat. In a whitewater kayak, you'll soon be able to tip far enough to put the coaming underwater, and to hold that position at will. Why would you want to do that? Because out on the water, the brace allows you to stay upright or

Low Brace. Power face of the blade is up and the elbows are above the paddle shaft.

A touring kayaker takes an opportunity to practice his low brace in calm water.

pull yourself up from extreme angles even when rough, powerful water around you would like to capsize you.

But what about when you are tired of that position, and yearn to be upright once again?

Meet the hip snap.

The hip snap is the logical extension of the wearing-the-boat trope: As hips go, so goes the kayak.

When you are ready to abandon the lean on your low brace and return to upright, cock the hips sharply and with authority. If you'd like, you can slap the water with your paddle, but with a firm rotation of the pelvic girdle, you'll soon find it unnecessary.

atop, the water — not that it matters. The water down there is just as dense, and equally ready to provide a helping hand.

Extend your right arm as you did with the low brace, but bring the left arm up so your fist is above the top of your head. With the power face of the blade parallel to the boat's side and dug into the water, sweep back and forth, again at about a 2-second-per-sweep pace.

When you first try it, the high brace may feel unstabilizing and, technically speaking, it is, since you are raising your center of gravity. In practice, though, the high brace is more than enough to keep you upright, and

THE HIGH BRACE

The way the high brace works differs from the way the low brace works in that the bracing blade is in, instead of

The classic high-brace arm position, for which it got its name. Since the paddle is naturally in this position each time you cross to stroke, it's the easier of the two braces to employ. And it's easy to convert a high brace into any other stroke.

Pros like rodeo champ Chris Selius — here playing in a surf hole on the Ocoee River, Tennessee — have so perfected their rolls that the maneuver seems effortless.

of reconfiguring for a low brace.

THE ESKIMO ROLL

This soon? you ask.

Why not? You've already aced its components — the hip snap, low brace, and high brace.

The Eskimo roll was invented as a survival technique. If you are, say, hunting narwhal off the coast of northern Greenland (where kayaks are still used for this pursuit), being upside down is a situation you wish to change as quickly as possible.

The roll's necessity is minimal in touring. If you keep an eye on weather conditions and avoid those in which you have no business being out, you can and probably will go through your boating career without capsizing one of

eminently more versatile than a low brace. In real-life boating, the paddle is naturally in the high position as you stroke, and it's easier and more convenient to turn that stroke into a high brace when a wave is trying to tip you, instead

High Brace. Power face of the blade is down and the elbows are below the paddle.

Eskimo roll performed in a touring kayak. 1) The roll setup: control blade is flat on the water, the paddle is on the surface and parallel to the kayak, the paddler is leaning forward. 2) The roll setup: same as before, only upside-down. 3) The sweep arcs away from the boat and the blade is close to the surface. 4) Upright once again. Notice that the paddler is now leaning back toward the rear deck.

these very stable boats. But if you do, it's nice to know you can turn upright effortlessly.

In whitewater kayaking, by contrast, capsizing will become a way of life as you hone your skills and begin to challenge the waves and the rapids. Playing hard in a kayak is one of the few games where you routinely and deliberately push *beyond* the edge of the envelope — and that's as it should be, because you know you can pop up with aplomb.

The physics of how the roll makes possible the seemingly impossible takes us right back to the brace. In a

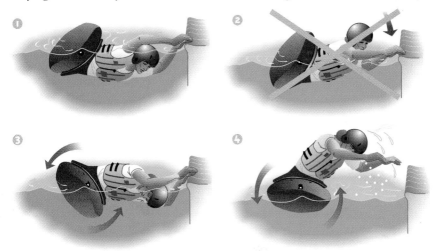

The Hip Snap. 1) While holding on to a fixed support, tilt the boat as far toward upside-down as possible. 2) The wrong way to hip snap: The kayaker's head comes up first, and she must use her arms to muscle up the boat. 3) The right way: The kayaker's head is the last part of the body out of the water; her hips are doing the work. 4) The power of the hip snap and the momentum of the rotating boat right the kayaker.

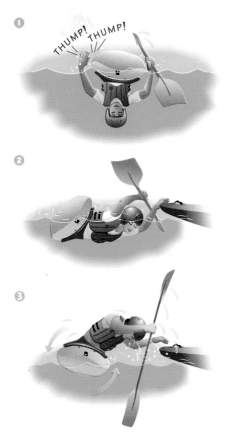

THUMP! THUMP!

The Eskimo Rescue. 1) Tap the hull to call in the rescue boat. 2) Grasp the bow of the rescue boat with one hand, retaining the paddle in the other. 3) Hip snap the boat upright.

waist-deep beside your boat. Maintaining your grip, flip yourself and the kayak to as near as upside down as you can. Drop your chin to your chest, so the top of your head is pointing toward the bottom.

Now: Hold your breath for a few seconds while you contemplate what you already know about weight distribution and center of gravity.

Visualize what comes next as cracking a whip. Centrifugal force dictates that moderate energy at the base of the whip — your hips — imparts greater energy to the "whip's" end — your head.

But first try what most first-timers try anyway: levering yourself up through upper-body strength rather than the hip snap.

It's a lot of work, and not particularly effective. Your head and shoulders are out of the water, but the boat is highly reluctant to come up.

Try it again, this time concentrating on the hip snap.

Now the hips are doing the work. The contributions of arms and shoulders are negligible. The head remains in the chin-tuck position, and is the last body part out of the water.

The mechanical reasons the head comes up last are intellectually obvious: Your hip muscles are more than strong enough to lift your head, but of course your neck muscles are not nearly up to the job of lifting your torso. Emotionally, however, in any situation in which a human is underwater, the urge is to get air-intake apparatus — nose and mouth — above

nutshell, you reach up to the surface with the paddle, perform an upside-down low brace, and bring yourself up on its firm and trusty support.

Warming Up for the Eskimo Roll

Before you attempt your first roll, two exercises will help you get ready.
EXERCISE 1: THE HIP SNAP. Lean over and with both hands hold the edge of a pool or the wrists of a partner standing

the surface pronto. Unless you overcome this psychological impediment,
you'll get that breath, all right — and
immediately find yourself back under
and in need of another.

Here's some psychotherapy. Before
you flip, remind yourself that, barring
spontaneous decapitation, your head
will follow your hips wherever they
lead. After that, forget your head alto-
gether. While you roll over, while you
pause to review your next move, while
you execute it — think *hips, hips, hips*.
As a tennis pro drills his focus into the
ball, drill yours into the pelvis. The
next thing you know, you'll be upright
and wondering how exactly you got
there.

EXERCISE 2: THE ESKIMO RESCUE.
Missing a roll becomes a lot more frustrating when you must wet-exit, drag
the boat to shore or poolside, empty it,
and reboard. The Eskimo rescue
avoids this hassle.

It's performed with the help of a
friend in a second kayak. She positions herself to form a bow-on T with
your boat.

If you don't make your roll, slap
on the side of your boat; this is your
signal that you are not going to make
another attempt (and you should consider one, especially if you managed to
get some air on the first unsuccessful
attempt). After the slap, run your hand
back and forth along the hull until you
feel the nose of the support boat. With
your now-powerful hip snap, grab hold
with both hands and pop yourself
upright, using the spotter's bow as you
did the poolside in Exercise 1.

There are situations where
knowing how to roll is unnecessary, and others where it won't
do much good.

Consider the Inuit narwhal
hunters of northern Greenland,
who wear neither dry suits nor
PFDs. The former would frighten
their prey, and the latter are
superfluous in water of a temperature in which survival is measured in minutes. So when the
outdoor writer Peter Stark went
kayaking near Qaanaaq,
northern Greenland, he was
rightfully apprehensive about
capsizing.

Seeking pointers on rolling
the unfamiliar native-style craft,
Stark was surprised to learn that
his host, Mamarut Kristiansen,
had never bothered to acquire
the skill at all. "What would you
do if you tipped over?" Stark
asked. The lifelong hunter considered the question as if it had
not previously occurred to him,
then replied, "Drown."

Roll 'Em

Rolling a kayak is like riding a
bicycle, in two ways. First, it looks
more difficult than it is. Second, preconceptions about its difficulty can
make learning more frustrating.

The Eskimo Roll. 1) Setup on your dominant-hand side (for most, the right). Lean forward and align the paddle parallel to the hull, with the power face of the forward blade flat against the water's surface. 2) Maintain the setup position as you roll the boat toward the paddle, while twisting to face in the same direction. Don't forget to hold your breath. 3) Count to three as you allow the boat to stabilize in the capsized position and you position the paddle. 4) Look up to see that your forward blade is flat against the surface. As you did with the low brace, sweep out and in an arc, moving the blade smoothly and with moderate speed. 5) As you complete the sweep, the brace naturally pulls you toward upright. Although you are levering yourself up on the brace, in practice, it feels as if the brace is doing the work. 6) Keeping the head down, hip snap with authority to complete the roll.

But the roll is also like hitting a major-league fastball out of the park; that is, it is heavily dependent on mechanics and technique. Nailing down the details of its sequence is the quickest path to success. I've seen a beginner flub dozens of rolls through failure to pay attention to the parts that make up its sum. I've also seen a person who'd never been in a kayak squat underwater in a pool, observe the maneuver, board the boat, and roll like a pro.

For visualization, the roll can be broken down into six steps. Take them in a relaxed mood and one at a time, and before you know it you'll be at the end of the path.

Note how the last step of the roll naturally leaves you in the high-brace position. This is a nice bonus. The odds are that the capsize was caused by turbulence or rapids. When you do come up, the water will be no more calm — and quite happy to flip you again. But you're ready for it, in trim to brace if necessary, or, better yet, to power-stroke and continue on your way.

THE EXTENDED-PADDLE ROLL

Also known as the Pawlata or "cheater," this is an intermediate step if the standard roll remains frustratingly elusive.

The execution is the same; the difference is paddle grip. The slip hand holds the blade by its end, and the control hand is at midshaft. The result is a longer and stronger brace upon

This paddler, at the midpoint of his sweep stroke, is about to execute his hip snap to right the boat.

TIPS FOR A SUCCESSFUL ROLL

1 Paddle diving occurs when, as you begin your sweep, your blade angle causes the edge to catch and dive down into the water. This is certain to take the wind out of the sails of your roll in short order. To make sure the blade is above the water's surface and lying flat against it, slap it and observe the splash that results. You'll soon be able to recognize from the splash's shape whether the paddle is in position.

2 Think "hips" — and forget the natural urge to get your head above water as soon as possible. During your 3-second concentration period, lay your cheek against the shoulder that will surface last, and keep it there until you've completed your hip snap.

3 Extend the forward arm as far as is comfortable without locking it — and at the same time keep the non-sweep arm's elbow tight to the rib cage.

4 Just as a weight lifter's spotter provides a tiny bit of help on that last bench press, some assistance from a partner standing by in the water can help you up on your first few rolls. For a paddle-diving problem, your spotter can adjust your blade and guide it through the sweep. Once you reach the point where you are *almost* successful, a spotter at the stern of the boat can provide a tad of extra torque to get you all the way up.

It won't take that many tries before you find yourself upright and looking back at your spotter to say, "Did you help on that one?" It's a pretty cool moment when she smiles and says, "Nope, you did that one on your own."

which to right
yourself.

Consider
the extended-
paddle roll a
temporary solu-
tion on the way
to learning its
standard cousin.
Its disadvantage
is that you must
change your
grip twice: in
the setup and
after the roll is
complete. This
is no problem in
flatwater prac-
tice, but in the
real world two
other factors
come into play.

First, if
your capsize is
not voluntary,
you must shift
your grip under-
water. It's not
difficult, but it
is something
else to think
about and

The sort of whitewater for which the high brace and (should it fail you) the Eskimo roll were invented.

requires a few extra seconds to do.
Second, although you do come up in a
brace position, it's an awkward one
that you'll have to lose while you shift
back to standard grip. As you're
feeling for the telltale, the water has
time to send you back for a second
visit with the fishes.

PADDLE STROKE BASICS

A few basic strokes and we're ready to hit the water.

Remember that rowboat at summer camp, with the oars set firmly in swivel locks? Steering was elemental: Pull on an oar and the boat turns away from that side of the boat.

Because your kayak paddle is not fixed, a stroke on a given side of the boat can turn it left, right, or not at all.

THE BASIC STROKES

Four families of paddle moves are more than adequate to get you under way: the power stroke, the forward and reverse sweep, the stern rudder, and the pry/draw.

The Power Stroke

For every ten times you dip blade to water, nine will involve a power stroke.

Once again, body mechanics come into play, and while arms and shoulders are important, hips continue to control the day.

Bending at the waist, lean forward and plant the blade at a comfortable extension. You're already gripping the shaft near the blade, so leverage is working for you. Smoothly draw the blade parallel to the boat's waterline.

As you complete the stroke, rotate the paddle to the other side, sliding the slip hand as you did in your dry-land lesson. Power-stroke on

Key points to remember when executing a power stroke: Keep the power blade immersed in and perpendicular to the water; plant the blade close to the side of the boat and keep it close through the pull; as you pull with the power hand, push with the opposite hand; twist your shoulder and torso through the stroke so that your arms aren't doing all the work.

the other side, and —

My gosh: You're moving, and in a straight line.

For the moment. Because of handedness, it takes experience before strokes are of equal power. When they are not and the boat seems to have

chosen a preferred direction on its own, the elementary solution is to cross over and stroke on the other side (bearing in mind that a pull stroke, if it does turn the boat, will do so in the direction of the side on which the stroke is executed).

Power Stroke. 1) Planting the control-side paddle. 2) Pulling (and pushing) through the stroke. 3) Planting the slip-side blade in preparation for stroking on that side.

The forward sweep is the best way to turn the boat in the opposite direction from the side on which you are paddling while maintaining full forward momentum.

A crossover in a kayak is easier and quicker than in a canoe. Neither hand need leave the paddle shaft, and the movement is more instinctual than thought driven.

But easier yet is to correct with a sweep stroke.

Sweep Strokes

In executing the sweep, the angle of your arms is the same as with the low brace, but your control-hand wrist is turned so the power face of the blade addresses the water. Assuming you are right-handed, reach forward and out on that side and stroke through the better part of a half-arc of a circle. The sweep will push you in the opposite direction

Forward Sweep Stroke. Making a broad sweeping stroke on one side of the kayak turns the boat in the opposite direction.

The Stern Rudder

The stern rudder is easily learned, but you should use it sparingly as a tool for steering correction.

To rudder, plant the blade to the rear of the cockpit — but remember your hydrodynamics. For the rudder to be effective, the boat must be moving forward against the rudder's resistance.

The disadvantage of the rudder is that it's a drag, literally speaking. The rudder retards forward movement. When possible and comfortable, use a forward sweep instead. You get steering control while maintaining momentum. And remember that momentum — movement relative to the water — is the key to stability. An injudicious stern rudder in the middle of a set of waves can leave you caught in the trough, with angry white stuff looming over your head and licking its chops in anticipation of chewing on you.

The faster the kayak is moving forward, the more responsive it will be to the stern rudder.

(that is, to the left), while still maintaining momentum.

A variation is the reverse sweep. Actually, it's a double-reverse, since it is done in a reverse manner and has the reverse effect: Sweep from stern to bow on the right side, and the kayak turns in that direction. A right-side power stroke followed by a right-side reverse sweep is one way to execute a 90-degree turn to starboard.

The Pry and the Draw

You've just entered your boat from a rock, a pier, or even the deck of a pool, and you want to get out into the water — or conversely, you want to reach a similar mooring to disembark.

You could push off with your paddle, or reach out and "grab" with it — and to be honest, that's what you'll

Rudder. Making a straight pry away from the stern at the end of a forward stroke turns the kayak to the power side.

Draw Stroke. Hold paddle in forward paddling position and turn your torso to the side. Plant the blade (power face toward the boat) 2 to 3 feet from the boat. Pull with the lower arm. Lifting up with your stroke-side knee will help keep the boat from tipping to the stroke side.

often do. But for more elegance and less chance to chip that expensive ash "stick," impress your partners with a pry or draw. These mirror-image strokes move the kayak sideways.

Pry and draw strokes are nice additions to your arsenal when quick course correction is in order — if, for instance, you are heading bow-on toward a rock or a floating ice chunk. Since you are already paddling forward, your paddle is in high-brace position. Slip the shaft 90 degrees so the blade is parallel to the boat's side, pry or draw as appropriate, and just like that you are back on course.

DO I NEED ALL THOSE STROKES?

If at this point you are wondering, "Do I really have to learn all this?," you might be surprised at the answer, which is —

No. You do *want* to learn all this. The only way to convince yourself that a

stern rudder, let's say, does its job is to practice until it feels natural (and this should take all of 10 minutes, incidentally).

But on the water, no kayaker says, "Hmmm. . .this situation calls for a power stroke followed by a sweep, and then a draw combined with a high brace. Now let's see… downside elbow in, upside blade raised with confidence, stroke 18.5 inches sternward. . . ."

Strokes, braces, and the Eskimo roll can — and should — be described in terms of technique, but don't let technique obscure utility. All have a single common purpose: compelling an upright kayak to go where *you want it* to go.

Consider strokes and braces as an all-you-can-eat buffet — and I'll be presenting more menu items when we concentrate on whitewater (see

Pry Stroke. Hold paddle in forward paddling position and turn your torso to the side. Plant the blade (power face toward the boat) next to the boat and pry it away from the boat by pulling with the upper hand and pushing gently with the lower hand.

The draw stroke can be very handy in whitewater when you need to change course in a hurry to avoid a rock or even a hole that looks too challenging.

you will employ.

You won't consciously think about why you made that choice until much later, when you are swapping lies with your mates about how you kept the boat trim in that boat-eating shore break.

For all intents and purposes, you've learned to "ride your bicycle." And like that bicycle, the old cliché maintains: Now that you've got it, you'll never forget how. You can, however, still fall off. Practice and mastery of some more advanced moves will help ensure that you don't.

Chapter 11). But the reason you don't have to know strokes and braces is that you will use them without thought.

Think of it this way: You can correct an overly powerful forward stroke by crossing over to a rudder. But, by and by, your instincts will remind you that before the crossover, your paddle is already in position for a reverse sweep — and that is the corrective

TOURING GEAR

In August of 1732, the Russian ship *St. Gabriel* anchored off what is now named the Seward Peninsula, at the westernmost point of mainland Alaska. The *St. Gabriel*'s commander was a scientist and cartographer named Michael Spriodovinich Gvozdev acting under commission from Czar Peter the Great, and as he glassed the mainland, he spotted an American approaching. Gvozdev's account notes that the visitor was in "a leather boat which had room for but one man. He was dressed in a shirt of whale intestines which was fastened about the opening of the boat in such a manner that no water could enter even if a big wave should strike it."

This earliest surviving written description of the kayak was glossed nine years later by Georg Wilhelm Steller, a naturalist who was a member of the expedition led by Vitus Bering, the Dane in service to Russia who gave his name to the eponymous strait. The boat's frame, Steller wrote, "is of sticks fastened together at both ends and spread apart by crosspieces inside. On the outside this frame is covered with skins, perhaps of seals. . .the boat is covered flat above but sloping towards the keel on the sides. . .on top is a circular hole, around the whole of which is sewn whale guts having a hollow hem with a leather string running through it, by means

kayaks made literally of skin and bones, hides stretched over animal skeletal parts. These of course were not, strictly speaking, touring kayaks, in the sense that Aleuts likely did not spend a lot of time in recreational sightseeing. Two hundred and fifty years ago, and possibly for as many as four millennia before, the kayak was a tool for fishing, hunting, and transport, and it still is for some northern natives.

CHOOSING A TOURING KAYAK

The touring kayak remains an elegant, efficient, and unchallengeably waterworthy craft today. Aside from the materials from which they are constructed, kayaks have not changed significantly since their formulation with regard to design, size, and utility.

Touring kayaks, like their whitewater cousins, come in many shapes, styles, and materials from fiberglass to rotomolded plastic to waterproof fabric stretched over a wood or aluminum frame (third from left).

of which it may be tightened or loosened like a purse. When the American has sat down in his boat and stretched out his legs under the deck, he draws this hem together around his body and fastens it with a bowknot. . . ."

The Aleuts encountered by Gvozdev and Steller were paddling

Stability

The typical tourer has good initial and directional stability. Some manufacturers do, however, offer models for the experienced boater that are narrower, faster, more maneuverable — and more tippy at rest. Advertising literature will indicate this; look for terms like "high performance."

Length

Most singles fall into a range of between 15 and 19 feet, with tandems running to 22 feet. Cargo room is one factor in choosing the length that is right for you. If day-tripping will be your principal activity, a lighter, shorter, less unwieldy boat provides more than enough carrying room. The ambitious boater with 7-day explorations in his future will appreciate the extra cargo space of a bigger boat, especially if he likes to eat well and sleep in padded, tented comfort.

Length affects two aspects of handling. First, longer boats have lower acceleration in relation to a given paddler's skill and strength. Acceleration is unimportant in open water, but if you are dodging rocks or trying to catch a wave, you'll have less "oomph" in a bigger kayak.

Second, once you have accelerated, length affects speed. A longer boat forms less of a bow-wave, which in turn means less friction — but only to a point. Clearly you would not get up much of a head of steam in a behemoth the length of a house trailer. The limit to the greater length = lesser resistance equation tops out at about 20 feet.

Furthermore, the equation is strictly true only when length is taken as an isolated factor — which it rarely is. For practical purposes, the extra

weight of gear will cancel reduced resistance. Let your boating plans and cargo-space needs guide you on the length issue.

Folding Kayaks

The pros and cons of boats fashioned of fiberglass, rotomold plastic boats, or hybrid materials are discussed in Chapter 2. The touring kayaker has another choice, the original recreational kayak known as the folding boat.

The folding boat is a direct descendant of the native kayak Gvozdev first observed, constructed on the same principles the Aleuts used. The animal skins have been replaced by a heavy-denier fabric, and the bone frame has given way to wood or interlocking aluminum poles.

Your choice of hull material is usually between canvas and Hypalon,

a synthetic rubber bonded to a cloth interior layer. Canvas "breathes," meaning that in warm weather the interior of your kayak will not become a crockpot-hot container; and because of its close weave, canvas is waterproof without the need for treatment with potentially polluting chemicals. Hypalon, on the other hand, is more resistant to abrasion.

Arguments on ideal frame material are more subjective, much like considerations of wood versus aluminum paddles. Just about the only verity applies to the special condition of cold water: Aluminum will take on the chill, wood will not. In maintenance and longevity, the differences are negligible.

In general, folding-boat owners make a number of arguments for their superiority, but for the average kayaker they come down to two. The first is a

A direct descendant of the Aleut kayak fashioned of animal skins stretched over bones, the folding boat replaces skins with waterproof fabric, bones with wood or aluminum poles. It is the ultimate portable boat: When the Feathercraft K-1 is broken down, it fits into a backpack.

matter of taste: Folding boats are by nature more flexible, and some kayakers find this an advantage in matching movement to wave action. The only way to determine if this suits you better than a rigid boat is to test both under the conditions in which you plan to kayak.

The second advantage of folding boats is more straightforward: When broken down, a folding boat is eminently transportable. Typically the components fit into two pack bags, one about $4^1/2$ feet by 1 foot, the other perhaps 2 feet by 2. These can be checked as airline baggage or tossed into a car trunk, and stashed in a closet during the off-season.

A few folding boats fit into a single bag, and their only advantage is to the ambitious boater/packer who

wants to carry a kayak into the backcountry. A single-bag boat can be backpacked, but you'd best be in good

GEAR TALK

SOME ASSEMBLY MAY BE REQUIRED

There's nothing quite like hiking a brand-new tent 10 miles into the backcountry — and forgetting the set-up instructions. Gee, who could have guessed this would be the first night in 6 months when it rained in the Mojave Desert?

The first place to put together your folding boat is your backyard. After your first success, break it down and start over again, until you can do it deftly and without consulting the manual. This precaution will save you a lot of waterside frustration, not to mention the derision of your hard-boat friends. When you become adept, assembly will take between fifteen and forty-five minutes, depending on the make and model of your boat.

If the manufacturer has not done it for you, labeling the parts can help; a simple color code will go a long way toward reminding you what goes where. Wrap each piece of the frame with a few inches of plastic tape, using a mnemonic scheme: red for "rear," blue for "bow," and so on.

Strawberry Island, San Juan Islands, Washington State. A group of sea kayakers prepare their craft and gear for another day of touring in the breathtakingly beautiful waters of Puget Sound.

enough shape to tote a minimum of 80 pounds.

Enhanced transportability should be the deciding factor in opting for a folding boat. You'll pay about 20 percent more than for fiberglass and about the same percentage in added weight, depending on the materials of the model and brand you choose. You'll give up little in durability: A quality folding boat will last decades if you keep the fabric clean.

However, many boaters who have used both rigid and folding kayaks think that with the latter there is a sacrifice in efficiency. Because they are heavier and slightly less sleek than their fiberglass or plastic cousins, folding boats require more effort to move them through the water.

TOURING EQUIPMENT

Depending on the brand and model, your touring kayak will be rigged with various accessories integral to the boat. If not, a retrofit may be in order. You'll also invest in gear necessary or useful for touring.

Rudders

Contrary to expectation, the rudder is not primarily a steering device, but an aid to stability and tracking.

The rudder is a fin bolted to the stern point of a touring kayak, and operated by foot pedals. When conditions dictate — in particularly forgiving water, for instance, or when launching or landing — it can be raised out of the water, according to one of two designs.

A retractable, or flush, rudder uses two lines for raising and lowering, and in the former position it lies flipped over and top-down against the stern deck. If there is a disadvantage to this configuration, it is that two lines provide greater opportunity for mechanical failure, though in a quality modern kayak, the chance of problems is low.

The operation of the non-retractable, or upright, rudder is simpler. A single line draws it out of the water and the line is secured; when released, gravity lowers the rudder. The slight downside here is that, as a function of the leverage provided by its extended position, it acts as an unwanted sail in windy conditions. This, too, is not a major concern, since in any serious wind you'll want the rudder in the water anyway.

Part of the kayaking population argues that a rudder is unnecessary, and several manufacturers offer rudders as an extra-cost option, or not at all. The argument goes like this: A well-designed boat tracks quite satisfactorily; a rudder adds weight (though not more than a few pounds); it hinders the roll; it's another piece of gear to maintain and which can fail; and you should have enough paddling skill not to need one.

The last has a touch of snobbishness to it, and I recommend that you choose a rudder-equipped kayak. For a premium of only about $100, its role in helping you to maintain your heading is occasionally invaluable. In a following sea that is not pushing in the

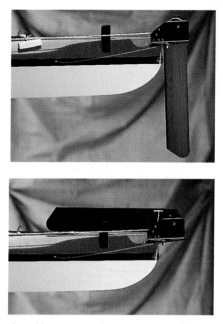

The rudder set-up on this Current Designs fiberglass boat is typical: the rudder is flipped up onto the deck (bottom) when launching and landing in shallow water by pulling a line inside the cockpit.

direction you wish to go, for example, only a masochist would deny a rudder's merit. The wave coming up behind you wants to grab your bow or stern and spin you. Your choice is to turn your rudder against the push or to wear yourself out in short order by vigorous, rapid paddling on one side of the boat.

Compass

The factory-mounted compass on the front deck of nearly all touring kayaks is a water-filled model, but make certain. If it was not water-filled when it left the manufacturer, it will be sooner or later.

For more on a compass's utility, see Chapter 8.

A simple, handheld pump strapped to the deck is the best choice for bailing out a kayak. The reliable, lightweight pumps are inexpensive and expel 6 to 10 gallons a minute.

quality control, this scheme is more friendly to the possibility of leaks.

British designers were the first to introduce the after-deck-mounted diaphragm pump, in versions operated by either hands or feet. It performs best when the amount of water to be evacuated is not great, because the volume it can handle per aspiration is low; don't count on it to empty a swamped craft.

A more common alternative in this country is a handheld pump. Choose one with an intake tube

Pumps

A capsize and wet exit is not the only event that might leave water sloshing about beneath your butt. Unlike the whitewater kayak, the touring model is most often a set of compartments (see "Hatches," page 73). Despite the integrity of modern construction and long enough to shove down the tunnel of your spray skirt, so you don't have to unsnap the skirt from the coaming. At around $30, this economical investment will expel 6 to 10 gallons a minute, and, unlike the deck-mounted model, can be moved among boats. Its disadvantage is that its use requires both hands.

Battery-powered electric pumps are fine when they work, and they usually do. The high-end models will even start up automatically when a pre-set level of in-hull water is reached. Bear in mind, though, that like all machines they have a Murphy's law mentality: They only fail when you need them most, and when they fail they are useless.

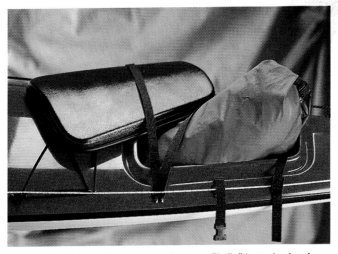

Watertight hatches provide easy access to storage "bulks" in touring kayaks. Still, it is prudent to store all gear and food in specially designed dry bags like the one shown. Notice the black deck lines for securing a pump, spare paddle, or other gear to the deck.

For run-of-the-mill bailing, don't neglect the sponge, handy for reaching nooks and crannies to sop up annoying intrusions caused by minor leaks and splashes. Synthetics are inferior to the ocean's home-grown product. Choose a good-sized hunk, secure it about the middle with 2 feet of line tied to a seat bracket, and tuck it into a cockpit cranny when not needed.

Deck Lines

Essentially permanently fixed bungees, deck lines provide two benefits. First, they are an additional grab point for use in the rescue of yourself or a paddlemate.

Second, deck lines secure the sort of gear that is nice to have instantly accessible, such as water bottle, chart, sunscreen, or granola bar.

Deck lines do a pretty decent job of countering the force of moderate boat-washing waves, but bear in mind that if you are upside down, significant turbulence might have put you there. Turbulence is a grabby, acquisitive pack rat; if it can get your stuff, it will.

So the rule is: Whatever you cannot afford to lose goes in the boat.

Hatches

A "bulk" — in the first, Middle English meaning of the noun — is simply a space. A bulkhead is the wall that defines that space, and a hatch — the part of the space with which we are most concerned, at least in the gear-up stage — is the way into that space.

In touring you'll regard your bulks as cargo area, but don't forget they also provide buoyancy. Given a kayak's ability to sink without added flotation,

Since it does not have the benefit of a wet suit to tough out the 28.6-degree water, the Antarctic cod has developed the ability to manufacture its own antifreeze. Unlike the ethylene glycol in your auto's radiator, which chemically lowers the freezing point, the peptides and glycopeptides produced in the liver of *Dissostichus mawsoni* alter the water's physics. "The fish breathes ice crystals, which normally want to grow," reports Charles Knight, senior scientist at the National Center for Atmospheric Research in Boulder, Colorado. "This makes them not want to grow." On a small scale, researchers have bioengineered one-celled organisms to manufacture the substance. The potential applications, according to Knight, range from increasing the storage life and texture of frozen foods to preservation during transport of human blood and donor organs.

this is no small consideration.

The first step in bombproofing your floatability is to stow gear in combination flotation/dry bags. Here is double duty at its most efficient: The weight of equipment is roughly offset by the air surrounding it, and, as a bonus, the dry bags keep the bulks from inundation in case of leaks.

Bulkheads can indeed leak, so recently some manufacturers have introduced touring kayaks with pods instead. Picture elongated plastic eggs sealed to the hatches, filling the rear compartment and fitting between your legs in the front.

Pods obviate the need for dry bags, and provide some supplementary stability and strength to the boat. But they also add weight (about 3 pounds per pod), and offer less cargo capacity. A compromise is a kayak with a pod in the front for items such as a sleeping bag that you absolutely do not want soaked, and a bulkhead in the stern space.

The hatches on a quality kayak are dependable — so don't depend on them. If rough water is a remote possibility, use web straps to batten down the hatches (often straps are a factory-installed feature).

Prudent touring kayakers secure a two-piece, breakdown spare paddle under the lines of the rear deck of their kayaks.

ANCILLARY EQUIPMENT

Even on a day trip, there's quite a laundry list of items you will wish to give some thought to toting along, many having to do with either navigation or convenience. I discuss their use in Chapter 8 and give checklists in Chapter 15.

Waterproof, inflatable dry bags keep gear and food safe, even if dropped overboard. The bags are designed to fit directly behind the seat, and can serve as additional back support.

Spare Paddle

Kayak paddles float, but that doesn't mean they can't be lost. A dump in a shore break or a turbulent tidal-current eddy line can leave you and your locomotion far apart; strong wind or current (see Chapter 7) can carry a paddle away far faster than you can swim. Also, careless contact with a rock or ice chuck can break blades.

If you have absolutely no reasonable expectation of encountering such conditions, a spare may be omitted, but prudently a spare is never a bad

---

TECHNIQUE TIP

KEEPING HIGH AND DRY

The less "wet" your clothing can get, the better off you are. Polypropylene is the standard, but pure plastic is an ecologically beneficial alternative. For years manufacturers have offered garments of woven plastic, and lately a number of them are turning recycled products such as bottles and six-pack rings into everything from sweaters to underwear. The process extrudes fibers that can be hair thin, and the garments woven from them are comfortable, utilitarian, and, while they can get wet, unlike cotton they will never be sodden. As a bonus, you'll keep a bit of nonbiodegradable detritus from the landfill. Such materials also include synthetic pile, synthetic sleeping-bag fill, and, in a pinch, wool. These will not absorb moisture, and will also release it while retaining the ability to keep you warm.

When possible, choose gear and supplies that are waterproof, or at least water resistant.

With food, look for sealed prepackaging, or repackage on your own in two Ziploc bags, one inside the other. If space is a lesser consideration, snap-lid containers work, but tape down the lids.

DID YOU KNOW

A touring kayak also makes a fine fishing platform, as well as a way to your favorite secluded secret spot. For the fisherpersons in the crowd, two bits of trivia with which to amuse your shore-mates, and one solid tip:

When your kayaking group becomes overly competitive in their pursuits of the elusive trout, remind them that fishing is "pryncypally for your solace and to cause the helthe of your body and specyally of your soule." This advice, included in 1496 in the first English-language book on the pursuit, *The Treatyse of Fysshynge with an Angle* (Middle English for "fishhook"), comes to us from Dame Juliana Berners, whose day job was prioress of the nunnery at Sopwell, Hertfordshire. A century and a half later, the better-known fishing commentator, Isaak Walton, borrowed from Dame Juliana for his *Compleat Angler* and incidentally proved her prescription correct. Walton continued to wet a line until shortly before he died in 1683, at the age of ninety.

idea. And as long as the group plans to stay together on the water, not every member need carry one; a two-piece breakdown paddle secured under the deck rigging for every three boaters will suffice on an average trip.

Dry Bags

These sealable rubberized sacks come in sizes from purse to large duffel, so choose among them to fit your boat's stowage spaces. Not only does a dry bag prevent sodden spare clothing when you make camp, but it provides flotation.

An axiom of backpacking is that a pack is a "bag full of bags." Apply the same principle to arranging gear in a dry sack. Eating utensils go in one ditty, toiletries in another, balm and bug juice in a third. Your boatmates may make fun of your Type A personality, but you'll be tucking in for forty winks while they are still looking for contact-lens solution.

Repair Kit

If you are piloting a non-plastic boat, invest in a patch kit. Buy the manufacturer's version specific to your kayak if available, but a generic kit from any well-stocked boating retailer is fine.

Add duct tape and copper wire; the many times they'll come in handy will convince you of the validity of the old adage relating necessity to invention. Where weight is an issue, don't take the whole spool. Instead, wrap what you expect to need around a pencil. Similarly, a small can of an all-purpose oil such as WD-40 will service your rudder mechanism, free a balky valve on your camp stove, and

Fishing for rock cod in Johnstone Straight, the passage of saltwater between the northwestern tip of Vancouver Island and mainland British Columbia, Canada. The 47-mile long, 1,000-foot-deep straight is teaming with sea life, including migrating salmon and the orcas (killer whales) that follow them.

prove itself useful for a variety of unanticipated annoyances.

A Swiss Army knife is a good all-purpose tool, but a Leatherman is a better one, because its features include pliers. Pliers are like dental floss: an unpretentious invention for which there is no substitute.

Rope

Lines are essential to every type of kayaking, for everything from tying your boat atop a vehicle to rescues, securing gear, and converting a couple of rain shells into a canopy. A kayaker somewhere in the world is jerry-rigging something with rope as you read this sentence.

The problem, though, is that ropes can turn on you, in seriously dis-turbing ways. The last happenstance you want if you are in the water is entanglement in what were supposed to be *safety* lines.

While there is debate, most instructors disavow unsecured bow and/or stern lines floating free while you are under way. If you do choose a bow line, coil and tuck it taut under deck lines, in a configuration that will free it quickly and without entanglement when you do need it.

RETROFIT VARIATIONS

Beyond the basic solo or tandem kayak, the options are dizzying — but most are designed to make touring accessible to more people. If you still find the boat a tippy or cumbersome proposition, they are worth a look.

Outriggers

Increase a kayak's beam by a factor of 2 and you have a rig that is more than twice as difficult to capsize; increase it by 3, and you can stand erect in the cockpit, or even take a stroll down the deck.

There are two ways to "cat" (turn into a catamaran) a kayak. One is the simple outrigger, a rigid float attached by extended arms to one or both (the latter makes it a trimaran) sides of the vessel.

The second is a framework that couples two kayaks side by side. Again, the result is a boat that rejects capsize in major ways; two tandem and catted kayaks have not only greater width, but the weight of paddlers in the each of the four corners.

Sail Mounts

Why paddle if you can harness the wind? Some tourers come with factory-installed mast sockets, or retrofit your own. Plug in, turn on, and tune out; let the zephyrs carry you along. As an added bonus, most mast fittings double as fishing-rod holders.

Kayaks as Rowing Platforms

If you're practicing for the Henley regatta, or are merely oar oriented, you'll find retrofits that suit you. Fixed seats combined with oar-lock racks are available to take on 9-foot oars, or you can choose a sliding seat that turns your kayak into a trainer.

O N
O P E N
W A T E R

Kayaking is like marriage. Some kayakers are faithful partners to the water they wed. They are happy and fulfilled with glassy-surfaced lakes and sheltered ocean bays, where gentle swells and 6-inch waves beckon like a welcoming lover.

Others are promiscuous philanderers with wandering eyes. Every new body of water turns them on. They pull the car over on the way to Grandma's house to contemplate the shoreline, wondering out loud about how they would approach that cliff break, the tidal bore over there. They say things like, "I'd seal-launch from that flat rock and brace into the last wave of the set, and be out of the soup before the next set comes in."

They drive their non-boating companions bananas.

But, for now, you'll choose flatwater for your first trip — and you are ready for it. You've mastered your equipment and your strokes; as long as you are comfortable with what you've learned so far, that's mastery enough.

Stop reading and go boating. *Bon voyage.*

After a while, the odds are that you'll eventually end up in the Lothario category. Most kayakers do; it's the nature of the beast. So let's take a look at some of the elements you'll encounter, and some novice and intermediate techniques for handling them.

LAUNCHING IN SURF

Many were the days in your youth when you visited Heavenly Bay and were disappointed by the barely-ankle-lapping waves denying you screech-and-holler fun. Now, though, you are pleased to find, on your frequent visits with your touring kayak, those placid conditions that make launching so easy.

But you show up one day to find that old Heavenly has turned Hellish. Here is significant surf, and it's you against it.

There are a couple of techniques for coping with it.

Assume a realistic situation that is challenging but doable: Ready to launch, you face breakers that you are willing to take on, but which are still higher than any you've encountered in your previously successful takeoffs.

Observe the waves from as high a vantage as is available: Does the barrier they present span the beach in either direction as far as the eye can see? This is unlikely; because waves break as a function of water meeting bottom, they will be less powerful — or nonexistent — where the bottom is deeper than the beach's mean depth.

In other words, look for a channel. The same outflowing current will form here. The law of averages, and the realities of the physical world, dictates that you won't find a perfect channel, but you should be able to see a line along which the waves' thump is well reduced.

Wave Types

Dumpers are breaking waves; as their bottoms scrape along, energy builds up that causes them to send it toward their bases. These are the pushy waves, the classic breakers in which overheated sunbathers love to frolic.

Spillers have their crests pushed back by the wind, and collapse upon themselves; in conditions ideal for launch, they are nearly swells, the

---

TECHNIQUE TIP

OPTING OUT

One way to avoid getting crunched by surf is to go home. As we'll discuss in the whitewater section (see Part III), you never have to do anything with which you're uncomfortable, and it's foolish to attempt the impossible.

"Impossibility" is a subjective combination of your abilities and confidence and the boat's capabilities to perform. If the biggest wave you've ever punched came up to your chest, and you are now facing 6-footers that give you a distinct case of the heebie-jeebies, maybe you should come back another day. We are back to physics here: Hit the face of that wave, and odds are you will not only go over, but a large and weighty volume of water will strive to keep you over.

Power stroking through surf, Point of Arches on the Pacific Coast of the Olympic Peninsula in Washington State. Maintaining stability depends on maintaining strong forward motion.

does in every kayaking situation, on presentation and forward motion. A boat that is moving in relation to the wave — and as you go through surf, the wave and you are moving in opposite directions — is more stable than a boat at rest.

Surf is a breaking swell. The forward energy of its movement is minimal except when it is in the act of breaking; otherwise it is merely bobbing along. The key to getting over it is thus to avoid the break.

This is observable before you challenge the waves, and partially observable when you are in them. The trough and the crest are both pieces of cake; it's being caught on the face that's the issue.

And if you are? Use what you've learned — and what works. A power stroke that draws you over the crest

white crest reduced to almost nothing.

Note also that surf waves come in sets, and lulls of varying lengths separate those sets. Get an idea of when the lulls occur, and time your charge to catch them.

When the only way out is punching the waves, stability depends, as it

A surf kayaker on the verge of planting a brace into the crest of a breaker.

before it breaks is effective if it beats the clock; so is a reverse stroke that pushes you back before the crest catches you. The former is superior — it keeps you moving forward. But the bottom line is to use whatever stroke does the trick.

LANDING IN SURF

Landing into surf that breaks against steep rock is another one of those situations best solved by avoidance. But there will be times that don't offer that option.

As with your launch, look for a channel. This has its problems; if the current is strong enough, it will bring you to a stop or, worse, push you out to the side and into the waves that you were trying to avoid in the first place.

There is a natural urge when you are separated from a tantalizingly close shore to just go for it. If your strokes are well honed, your roll bombproof, your braces firm, your gear completely secured, and there are no potentially head-bashing obstructions below the surface, paddle on. Sometimes you might have to. But when you do, there are a couple of cautions that will make success — in an upright position — more within your grasp.

What you have on your mind in this case is surfing and pearling. The former has to do with pleasantly staying atop the water; the latter with the unpleasant experience of auguring into it.

Surfing

Surfing is not necessarily a *faux pas*; if you've acquired the necessary skills and confidence, riding a touring kayak across the face of a breaking wave is exhilarating. When you pull it off and reach the shoreside foam, it is considered perfectly accept-

Surfing big breakers can be great fun, as this kayaker demonstrates as he turns his boat across the wave by ruddering with his paddle blade.

able to look over your shoulder, thumb your nose at the waves to your back, and go "Nyah, nyah."

Pearling

If the waves are saying "Nyah, nyah" to *you*, you may well have pearled. The term refers to burying your bow deeply enough into the water that its rush and volume upend the stern. The effect is that your front end stops short while your rear keeps going. You can imagine the result: After you kayak for a while in a distinctly vertiginous vertical position, you kayak in an upside-down position.

Soft Landing

Assuming you couldn't find a sheltered stretch of shore without breakers, resist the urge to rush; sit off-shore for a while to assess the situation as best you can. One of your problems is that

from your vantage — low and behind the breaking waves — it's difficult to judge their strength. One sensible

?

DID YOU KNOW

In any powerful hydraulic, including those in river rapids, don't use a high brace. A sharp riptide line, for example, can jerk your blade down without warning, and if this occurs and your opposite arm is held too high it will be snapped even higher, with the potential for a dislocated shoulder. Keep the opposite elbow close to the rib cage to avoid this common kayaker injury.

High bracing into the foam of a breaking wave. You'll have to employ this move when launching and landing through surf. Notice the hand pump securely fastened to the rear deck.

option is to let the strongest, most experienced member of your group go first. Once she's ashore, she can give you some notion of the route of least resistance.

If that's not an option, you must venture on. The forward-moving section of the wave on which you want to hitch your ride is its forgiving backside, immediately behind its crest. This section of each breaker will push you forward for a bit, then reject you

---

TECHNIQUE TIP

INFORMATION PLEASE

To help make your launch and landing as easy as possible — no surprise here — launch from and land where there is an accommodating spot. Guidebooks are available for many popular sea-kayaking venues; some are listed in Sources & Resources. Local inquiry is another good source of information. Try paddling retailers, the office of the coast guard or harbormaster if there is one, or, in a pinch, look in parking lots for vehicles with local license plates on the bumper and a kayak on the roof.

as if you were the runt of the litter. From the trough in which you are left, back-paddle up the face of the next wave before it begins to break. You don't want to get picked up by a wave and propelled shoreward until you are ready.

At some point, however, you must commit yourself to riding a wave or you will be progressing only just so far and then back-paddling out of harm's way indefinitely. When you commit, you'll feel yourself (and your boat) surged forward toward impact with the beach. Before you know it, your kayak will have turned side-on to the shore, and the next wave will broach you. You must instantly head away from shore and plant an aggressive high brace into the foaming top of the oncoming breaker. Hold onto your brace. You're in the froth inside the breakers, and close to shore. Get out of the boat as quickly as possible and treat yourself to a serving of your favorite beverage. You've earned it, for while you may not have landed with style, you've safely landed.

WIND

Nearly all bodies of open water large enough to attract kayak exploration are regularly visited by wind. These breezes are usually either onshore (blowing toward the shore) or offshore.

On a hot cloudless summer day at lakeside or beach, you've probably noticed that afternoon onshore winds are more likely than not. If on the next day the weather happens to turn cool,

the winds are reversed.

This occurs because ground is a less efficient heat reservoir than water; that is, its circadian temperature swing is greater, since it both heats and releases heat more quickly.

In the case of the onshore breeze, as the land mass reaches its greatest warmth late in the day, the air above it rises and cooler air moves in to fill the void. The offshore breeze is a mirror image: The temperature-stable air over the water remains warmer than the air above the quickly-heat-releasing ground.

This is a simple description of *convection* winds. However, wind in the natural world is not a neat, reliable, or even completely predictable machine. Convection winds can come in from every point on the compass rose — and shift whimsically and rapidly. Wind has a million tricks.

Two commonsense precautions are listening to the weather report, and looking around. A major front on the western horizon means thinking about postponing your trip if you are ashore, or getting ashore if you aren't.

Wind generally becomes a matter of serious concern, and potential peril, only if you regularly cruise water that is either vast enough to take you beyond sight of shore or located in any area subject to frequent and radical weather shifts. Otherwise, most winds you'll meet while under way (or will want to meet) are a 3 or less on the Beaufort scale. (See pages 86 and 87.)

Wind at these magnitudes is more an irritation than a danger to the touring kayaker. It's frustrating when a headwind cuts your 4-knot cruising speed in half, and early in your kayaking experience you may have the feeling that the wind wants to knock you over. It may want to, but it's not

very good at it.

The one orientation to avoid is broadside to the wind, or perpendicular to its force. A kayak in wind is at its best trim when the wind is at the boater's back. Running into the wind,

BEAUFORT SCALE OF WIND SPEED

Beaufort Number or Force	Wind Speed			World Meteorological Organization Description	Effects Observed at Sea	Estimating Wind Speed	
	Knots	mph	km/hr			Effects Observed Near Land	Effects Observed on Land
0	under 1	under 1	under 1	Calm	Sea like a mirror rises vertically	Calm	Calm; smoke
1	1-3	1-3	1-5	Light Air	Ripples with appearances of scales; no foam crests	Small sailboat just has steerage way	Smoke drift indicates wind direction; vanes do not move
2	4-6	4-7	6-11	Light Breeze	Small wavelets; crests of glassy appearance, not breaking	Wind fills the sails of small boats which then travel about 1–2 knots	Wind felt on face; leaves rustle; vanes begin to move
3	7-10	8-12	12-19	Gentle Breeze	Large wavelets; crests begin to break, scattered whitecaps	Sailboats begin to heel and travel at about 3–4 knots	Leaves, small twigs in constant motion; light flags extend
4	11-16	13-18	20-28	Moderate Breeze	Small waves 0.5–1.25 meters high becoming longer; numerous whitecaps	Good Working breeze, sailboats carry all sail with good heel	Dust, leaves, and loose paper raised up; small branches move
5	17-21	19-24	29-38	Fresh Breeze	Moderate waves of 1.25–2.5 meters taking longer form; many whitecaps; some spray	Sailboats shorten sail	Small trees in leaf begin to sway
6	22-27	25-31	39-49	Strong Breeze	Larger waves 2.5–4 meters forming; whitecaps everywhere; more spray	Sailboats have double reefed mainsails	Larger branches of trees in motion; whistling heard in wires

while it does retard your speed, is nearly as stable an alignment.

Unfortunately, frequently neither of these positions will coincide with the directions you had in mind to take. Here's where ferrying comes in.

Ferrying

A ferry takes your kayak diagonal to the wind, and you'll use it to move from an area of bigger waves to calmer water and to cross currents. At the same time, the ferry helps stabilize

Beaufort Number or Force	Wind Speed			World Meteorological Organization Description	Estimating Wind Speed		
	Knots	mph	km/hr		Effects Observed at Sea	Effects Observed Near Land	Effects Observed on Land
7	28-33	32-38	50-61	Near Gale	Sea heaps up, waves 4-6 meters; white foam from breaking waves begins to be blown in streaks	Boats remain in harbor; those at heave-to	Whole trees in motion; resistance felt in walking against wind
8	34-40	49-46	62-74	Gale	Moderately high (4-6 meters) waves of greater length; edges of crests break into spindrift; foam is blown in well-marked streaks	All boats make for harbor, if near	Twigs and small branches broken off trees; progress generally impaired
9	41-47	47-54	75-88	Strong Gale	High waves (6 meters); sea begins to roll; dense streaks of foam; spray may reduce visibility		Slight structural damage occurs; slate blown from roofs
10	48-55	55-63	89-102	Storm	Very high waves (6-9 meters) with overhanging crests; sea takes a white appearance as foam is blown in dense streaks		Seldom experienced on land; trees broken or uprooted; considerable structural damage occurs

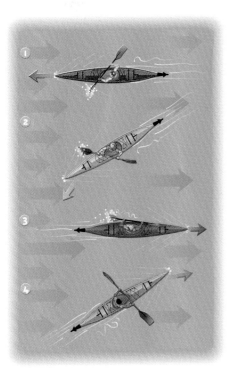

Ferrying Basics. 1) Paddling into the wind 2) Ferrying into the wind 3) Running with the wind 4) Ferrying with the wind. Large arrows at left signify wind or current direction.

A greater angle speeds the ferry but increases the opportunity for the hydrodynamic to push the kayak over.

Since the tendency of the water movement is to swing your bow and increase the angle you've chosen, most of your strokes will be on the side from which the wind- or water-power is coming. Upper-body strength does help in the ferry situation, but you need not be a broad-shouldered behemoth to pull it off. A smooth, regular rhythm should overcome any failings in the power department.

If bracing and leaning is required to keep the boat in trim and upright, use low strokes to reduce the risk of shoulder dislocation. You may also want to turn your paddle blade to about halfway between stroke and brace position, so you can switch to the latter more quickly when it's needed. Use this paddle support to "edge" the side of the hull toward the oncoming force, and your stability is increased that much more.

Getting Personal with Wind

The question of how much wind you should try to handle is its own answer: How much wind do you want to handle?

Your judgment should depend first on the "pucker factor." Indeed, this applies to all the challenges you accept or decline, in a touring or a whitewater kayak. A guide to the decision is always: If it doesn't feel like fun, don't do it.

But another important considera-

your boat as you make your way through these occasionally tricky waters.

The three keys to a successful ferry are correct boat orientation; a steady assertive stroke; and bracing combined when necessary with leaning into the wind, waves, or current flow.

Bearing in mind that the kayak will move in the direction the bow is pointing, your angle from direct head-on address will be about 30 degrees, give or take 10. The optimal orientation within this range is a matter of experience, feel, and prevailing conditions. Here is yet another kayaking trade-off:

The amount of wind and size of waves you tackle should depend on your gut reaction to your ability and the temperature of the water and air. When in doubt, wait for a calmer day.

tion is the general characteristic of the water, aside from wind. A dump in the ocean within sight of Costa Rica's Manuel Antonio beach means a refreshing swim; one in Alaska's Kotzebue Sound on the Arctic Circle puts you a few steps from fatal hypothermia. Remember, too, that once you put out in the wind, at some point you'll have to get back to land. It's one thing to launch through 6-inch foam, and another to beach through 6-foot breakers.

WAVES

Wind is one source of waves, and obstacles — such as the shore that forms those 6-foot breakers — are a second. The third is water moving against itself, from currents, tides, whirlpools, and similar phenomena.

The morphology and hydrodynamics of these waves, and the many forms they take, are endlessly varied, endlessly intricate, endlessly fascinating — well, you get the idea: endless. Instead of physics, let's look at where you'll find waves, and what to do with them when you do.

The Wind-Wave Connection

At the wind force that we've set as the limit of our challenge for now, a Beaufort 3 (8-12 mph), open-water whitecaps are a foot high at most. You'll feel their push, but you'll quickly be ferrying them without any real trouble.

Shore waves, given a specific stretch of beach, are more variable with tide and wind changes. Your defense here is threefold: Be aware of the tide schedule for the day of your trip; check the wind forecast (but remember that forecasts can be wrong); and learn, by either observation or local inquiry, how your put-in and landing spots usually react to tides and wind.

Don't neglect to take into consideration the planned length of your trip, and wave changes that might occur while you are gone. For example, consider a beach break that slopes gently out to the distant low-tide line, but steepens appreciably at the high-tide line. A 6-hour trip that begins at low tide gives you easy water at launch but, all other factors being equal, serious crashers to be negotiated at landing.

Waves in Tidal Streams

Waves that are created by moving water are challenging at best and non-boatable at worst. On the lower half-dozen miles of the Severn River in southwestern England, for example, under the right conditions, tidal streams are so powerful that they have

---

T E C H N I Q U E   T I P

SWELLS

Swells are waves that don't break (or haven't yet broken), rolling undulations caused by a disturbance some distance away. While they do have a forward-movement component — think of the concentric ripples blossoming from a penny dropped in a wishing well — most of their energy goes into raising and drawing down the water's surface.

The mechanics of a swell are intuitive: The disturbance (whether a storm a hemisphere distant and on the other side of the ocean, or the wake of a speedboat) pushes down an area of water, meaning the adjacent area must bulge. Gravity draws the bulge down below the mean surface into a trough. After that, the former trough rebounds to form the next bulge.

A 10-foot swell sounds threatening, but it's actually a kick. The touring kayak under which it passes rises majestically to the summit, providing a panoramic view. The kayak and you are lowered into the trough, and though water rises well above you fore and aft, it presents no threat of crashing atop you. A moment later, you catch the up elevator, and are again king of the mountain.

One caveat: The swell that is benign in deep open water is less so if it is nudging you toward shore, cliff, or reef. When close to water's edge, use that moment of elevation to look around and check to see if swells are turning to breakers in the near vicinity.

been ridden on a surfboard.

Tidal streams are caused by the hydrodynamic equivalent of trying to shove 100 pounds of flour into a 50-pound sack. Tides entering a constriction must cause radical changes in water level, volume, and speed. The

Paddling into a strong wind can cut 2 or more knots from your speed. Add to wind increasing wave action, and you have some excitement — and plenty of exertion. On larger waves, paddle hard on the downward slope and ease off on the upward slope.

result is similar to standing waves on a whitewater river, with a few added features. The water forming the wave is moving in the opposite direction of both water beneath it and water to either side of it, depending on the configuration of the banks. Expect to encounter overfalls, in which water rushing over rock ledges can produce "holes" (see Chapter 12); "stopper" waves too pushy and steep to climb over; and powerful eddy lines.

Experience and familiarity with the techniques discussed in the whitewater section (see Part III) are highly recommended before attempting a tidal stream, and even then the disadvantage in reduced maneuverability of the bigger touring boat will demand your most flawless technique. Until you are more than proficient, your best bet is to know where tidal streams and waves occur, and give them a wide berth.

Under, Over, and Through the Wave

A wave, whether a wind-whipped whitecap or a shoreside breaker, is a swell that is transferring its energy from the vertical plane to the horizontal. Wade into the surf, await a 3-footer, and at the last moment dive through its base; down there, the resistance is slight.

Now stand erect and let the next

?

DID YOU KNOW

The highest coastal wind ever recorded was 207 mph on March 8, 1972 at Thule Air Force Base, located on Greenland's west coast.

Low Brace Into a Wave. Counter the wave's attempt at capsizing the boat by both planting a low brace into the face of the wave and hip-rolling toward it.

one hit you in the chest. You are knocked butt over teakettle and digging sand out of your ear.

It is possible to get under a wave in a kayak, but it's an advanced move: With the boat abeam, capsize deliberately and let the wave wash over you, then roll up. If the water is warm and your roll is bombproof, this works fine. If not, you'll prefer to go over the wave.

In breaking whitecaps that rise up in open water, take them directly into their face, paddling hard to punch your kayak through. You can do this backwards with reverse strokes if you involuntarily find yourself stern-to, but, given the choice, practically and

DID YOU KNOW

Canada lays claim to the greatest regular tidal fluctuation. In the Bay of Fundy, between Nova Scotia and New Brunswick, low and high tide in the spring vary by an average of $47^1/2$ feet. At the other end of the scale is the Pacific island of Tahiti, whose coast experiences almost no tide at all.

psychologically it helps to see where you are heading.

Getting Sideways

In real-life circumstances, there will be occasions when you get side-on, by either your choice or the wave's. At these times, the low brace is your savior.

Bracing into a wave is counterintuitive. The force you feel is trying to turn you over away from the wave, and the urge is to seek support on that side. The problem is, a brace on the off-wave side is going to be a 98-pound weakling, and the wave is sure to end up turning you over. The "upstream" low brace (see illustration above) by contrast, takes advantage of equilibrium instead of futile brute strength — and it works.

TIDES AND CURRENTS

Tides and currents are exclusively the concern of the seagoing kayaker, and both the literature and the hard information on them are extensive (see Sources & Resources). Their effects and behaviors, alone and in combination, are also extensive — nearly to the point of being infinite. I'll leave the technical aspects to more detailed treatment, and concentrate on the information you'll want in hand, and what to do with it.

All you need to know about the "why" of tides you learned in grammar school: They are a function of the gravitational pull of the sun and the moon, and vary in magnitude according to those bodies' alignment or lack thereof. A tide is water moving up or down.

A current is water that is moving within fairly well discernible boundaries; a good way to think of a current is as a "river" whose banks are relatively still water instead of solid ground. Mega-currents such as the Gulf Stream are a function of prevailing winds and varying water temperature. The currents you can expect to find in open water usually result from tide action and the topology of either the sea bottom, shore features, or a combination of both.

While you're concentrating on understanding waves and tides when paddling through them out on the ocean, don't forget to take tides into account once you're back on land. Be sure to make camp well above the high tide line.

Tide and Current Tables

Unless you are intimately familiar with the area in which you plan to kayak, your basic information package should begin with a tide table, showing for a given shore point the time and height of high and low tides (usually four a day, but occasionally three; the mean time between tide changes is about 6 hours and 15 minutes). Note that the height figure is not written in stone; it's a prediction from the National Oceanic and Atmospheric Administration (NOAA), albeit a generally accurate prediction.

Tide tables are a bit more complex than they appear at first blush. The reference point is usually a municipality, so you'll find as part of the document a list of up- and downshore secondary points giving their "correction factors," a number to be added to or subtracted from the primary-point figures. If conditions are benign and your launch is less than five miles from the primary reference, you can ignore the correction if you wish, though it's easily made.

A current table is similar. Its heading gives the compass direction of the flow at flood and at ebb tides; the entries show the times they occur, the current's maximum predicted speed, and the time of slack. "Slack" is the point at which the current comes to a halt before reversing direction. Note that while slack is related to tide changes, not every current goes slack exactly at the moment of low or high water; differing shorelines and sea floors can greatly affect timing.

Tidal Tricks

Aside from tides' potential effect on shore-wave conditions and tidal streams, try not to let a tide change play its favorite practical joke on you.

Remember that the water from which you land is going to be elsewhere when you re-launch. Make camp below the high-water mark, and at 3 a.m. you'll be sleeping with the fishes while your boat departs for regions unknown. By the same token, if your next-day launch is at low tide and the slope of the bottom is gradual, you could have a long carry — of boat and of gear — down to where the ocean has removed itself.

Current Events

Currents, on the other hand, are strictly an on-water concern. They can be your best pal if they flow in the direction you have in mind, but remember that the type of current I'm treating here — as opposed to the Gulf Stream — reverses itself roughly in concert with the tides.

In sea where currents play a major role, supplement your current table with a current map (for such areas, one has usually been published). In combination with the table, the map is a valuable aid in planning your trip to exploit rather than fight with currents. Hitchhiking a ride with a current is a pleasure, especially after a stretch of paddling without assistance; you have the happy feeling that you and the ocean are convivial collaborators. Paddling against a current is highly frustrating. An opposing current at a given speed will slow you much more than a wind of the same velocity. If your paddling speed is 3 knots, you'll make merry headway against a 3-knot zephyr. But a 3-knot current will stop you dead, and a 4-knot flow will tow you backwards.

N A V I G A T I N G
O P E N
W A T E R

Whitewater river kayaking has one great advantage over touring: It's hard to get lost. Rivers flow inexorably in one direction; they are collaborators in getting you to where you want to go.

Touring on open water offers more alternatives on where you might end up — and in the best of all worlds, that should always be where you *planned* to end up. The natural inclination is to use shore features for landmarks, and you'll certainly be doing so. But there will come that time when you beach at the forked tree that marked your put-in and discover that *your* forked tree is across the lake. Oceanside points of reference — a distinctive rock, for

example — can simply disappear from view under the incoming tide.

Your three basic tools for navigation are a compass, charts and maps, and the knowledge to make use of them.

COMPASS

If your touring kayak did not come with a manufacturer-installed compass, mount your own. Pick a point far enough forward along the centerline of the deck where, given your height, you can glance down at it with minimal movement of your eyes from the horizon line. Not that you have to be staring alertly straight ahead at all times; this is simply a read easily at the mounting distance.

CHARTS

Detailed nautical maps are published by the National Oceanic and Atmospheric Administration (NOAA) and some private cartographers. The most convenient source is a boating retailer in the area of your trip, although NOAA maps can be ordered directly (see Sources & Resources). Some charts are available on waterproof paper, but a helpful accessory is a clear-plastic zippered map case; it will

Planning a kayaking trip, Puget Sound, Washington State. Charts, maps, and compass — and a working knowledge of their use — are the three basic tools of navigation.

matter of convenience.

Make certain that the compass is mounted level, and affix it with an adhesive that won't be antagonistic to your boat's material; your best course is to check with your outfitter. Last, choose a compass that is large enough to be

display about a half square foot of your folded chart, covering a varying area depending on scale, but at least a dozen square miles. The case also allows you to double-secure your chart by sliding it under your deck bungees.

United States Geological Survey

topographical maps chart inland water and coastal land areas. They are a nice adjunct to charts, and fun to have along if you plan to hike during stopovers, or even if you're just a bit of a map freak. One caution: USGS maps are not always current, and you'll want to check the date (look in the bottom border) of the original survey and any revisions made since then. If the latest revision is 20 years old, that trail to a high-country lake may be long overgrown — or, just as bad, the lake may now be the sight of a mega-resort served by a superhighway.

THE EDUCATION OF A YOUNG NAVIGATOR

symbols, and circles to be dazzlingly discouraging. Chart No. 1 contains a detailed key for deciphering them.

Alexander Pope's admonition that "A little learning is a dangerous thing" applies in spades to piloting. There's no such thing as a three-paragraph crash course, so I'll leave it to you to seek counsel from Burch's text, supplemented by some hands-on lessons from

Paddling toward "The Churches," a set of small sea stacks in Tenacatita Bay on the west coast of Mexico. Such landmarks can be useful for ranging, a basic form of navigation in which you line up two distant objects to stay on a set course.

Technical navigation is a complex subject, though not difficult to learn and even fascinating if you've got any sort of orderly mind-set. Its nuances, however, could fill a book, and they have — it's *Fundamentals of Kayak Navigation*, by David Burch (see Sources & Resources), and it should be part of your library if you plan to tour open water.

Also order NOAA's "Chart No. 1." The first time you confront a chart, you'll likely find the lines, numbers,

a seasoned seaperson. But there are a few techniques — and a few cautions — that will aid your navigational efforts.

A solid footing in navigation isn't enough to get you where you want to go if you don't add planning and flexibility. This is especially important if you are touring from point to point, with one or more overnights and perhaps an eventual take-out distant from your original launch.

To get from your put-in point (A), near the road in the the town of Trosclair, to the beach on Sybil Island (D), you have an opportunity to plot two compass courses and use ranging at least twice.

For the first leg, follow a course of 189° magnetic from A to B. To determine your arrival at point B, check the shoreline on your right side. When Janie Point and the south edge of Burtch Island line up, you're there, and it's time to change your course to 238° magnetic for the 6-mile second leg to D, the beach at Sybil Island.

Ranging will also pinpoint C. You have gone about halfway when, to your left, the western edges of Greg Rocks and Robert Henry Island are aligned. At the same time, looking to your right and then quickly to your left, you are mid-way between Burtch and Karen Rock.

Approaching your destination (D) on Sybil Island, correct for drift or minor navigational errors by aiming directly between the island's two summits. As an additional visual aid as you come in, you can see Peter Island to your left and the three big rocks to your right.

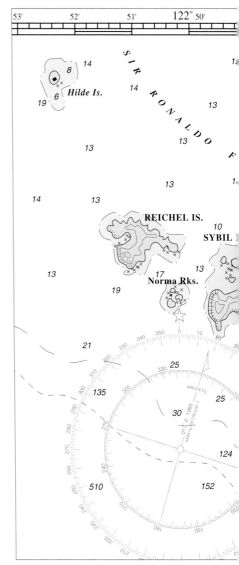

Planning is deciding how far you will travel and by what route. Flexibility is the willingness to change your planning.

And you will be changing your plan. The equation of how long a given voyage will take has so many factors that it can never be solved with the precision of an algebraic formula. These factors include the natural (and only approximately predictable) phenomena we've looked at, including tide, current, weather, and wind, but also human variables that play an equally significant role.

Unless you model yourself on Captain Bligh, your touring party is only as fast as its slowest member — and he or she is not necessarily the least experienced. Equipment breakdown, fatigue resulting from a bad night's sleep, or even a lousy attitude will throw you off schedule. Benign factors affect your schedule, too.

Should you discover a gorgeous cove with bath-warm swimming, you've got a swell reason to convert your 10-minute rest stop into a 2-hour laze.

Deriving an approximate solution to the planning equation involves a four-part approach. First, estimate

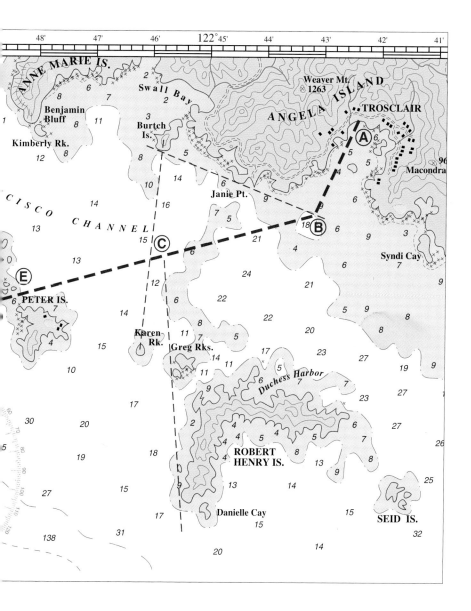

your party's average hourly speed; 3 knots is typical. Second, adjust this speed according to conditions. Third, based on the first two steps, derive a realistic guess on how long it will take to get from A to B. Fourth, increase that time by 25 percent.

With this planning philosophy, flexibility is built in for 90 percent of the trips you take. For the other 10 percent, it serves as training, in that it habituates you to the plans-are-made-to-be-changed mind-set. In a worst-case scenario, you are comfortable

Long before charts, sextants, and all the other tools of modern navigation came into use, skilled mariners (the Vikings and Polynesians preeminent among them) depended on common sense and their wiles. Two of their techniques still have applicability when you are, respectively, out of sight and in sight of shore features.

Dead Reckoning

It's like the dew point: A couple of words you've heard all your life — but what the heck do they mean?

Navigating the spectacular — but also tricky — waters of Penobscot Bay along the Maine Island Trail. Sea kayaks should be rigged with a compass affixed to the front deck for quick reference when reading charts.

with the idea of putting in to shore; tomorrow is another paddling day. In the *worst* case, when shore is not an option and nature is being naughty, you have trained yourself to concentrate on riding out the conditions, instead of on how your schedule is being messed up.

The connotative definition of "dead reckoning" is "guesswork," and to a degree that describes the denotative definition. For the kayaker, dead reckoning is an estimate of direction and distance covered, based on speed and compass heading.

Dead reckoning comes into play

on the occasions when you are out of sight of land — and of landmarks — for a significant leg of the voyage. This might occur in a crossing of open water, or result from reduced visibility caused by mist or fog.

To dead-reckon, you hold a particular compass course for a period of paddling time. Say you are far enough away from shore that you cannot see the beach, and you wish to make port at a specific point down shore. Assuming that you chose a heading roughly parallel to the shoreline, and assuming that your estimate of your paddling speed is reasonably precise — and that's a lot of assuming — a 90-degree turn made at a given time based on your speed estimate should land you about at the site for which you were aiming.

Dead reckoning is an art informed by craft. It's useful in kayaking only under the twin conditions in which the accuracy of your estimate of speed is matched by close attention to the direction you are speeding toward. The second factor is easy — you have kept an eye on your compass, right? The first is more ephemeral and experience oriented. On an average leisurely paddle, you know that you can make about 3 knots. Factor in wind and current as retarding effects, and recalculate for true speed.

To improve your dead-reckoning skills before you need to use them, get in the habit of measuring your speed

KNOT CRAFT

A "knot" is, strictly speaking, a measure of speed rather than distance; it equates to nautical miles per hour. A nautical mile, incidentally, is 1 minute (1') of latitude, or $1/21,600$th of the earth's circumference. Say what? Okay: A nautical mile is about 1.15 times a standard mile.

What this means to you is that for shorter trips in calmer water, you can consider the nautical mile to be roughly the distance your car odometer ticks off when traveling down the highway. Most sea trips, though, will rarely proceed in an unimpeded straight line. Other factors being equal, take the conservative tack and assume that a 3-knot pace will advance you 2 miles or a little better for each hour of paddling.

This "fudge factor" — how much to add to your estimated travel time — is a judgment call, but one in which the upside is greater than the downside. After all, the worst thing that can happen is you arrive early — with more time to set up camp in daylight, break out the crackers and Brie, and tell fibs about the humongous wave you surfed to shore.

DID YOU KNOW

During a shoreside lunch break on a recent kayak tour, our party — intellectuals that we are — found ourselves musing on the question Archimedes posed around 250 BCE: How many grains of sand would it take to fill the earth and the heavens?

The solution struck us as too daunting, so we considered instead the beach on which we lolled, about 50 yards long, 20 wide, and — for the sake of the discussion — one yard deep, for a volume of 1000 cubic yards. Painstakingly lining up granules, we estimated 30 to the inch. A few minutes of mental gymnastics revealed that this bit of the earth and heavens contained about 1.26 trillion grains of sand.

Unwilling to take this result on faith, several of us decided to count them, until cooler heads pointed out that at one grain a second, it would take about 40,000 years. So we finished the chocolate chip cookies and set out through the surf instead.

over courses whose length you know, and under varying degrees of wind, waves, tide, and current. When the dead-reckoning occasion arises, plug into your calculation your typical pace for the specific conditions.

Dead-Reckoning Considerations

Attention to two other factors will increase the accuracy of your dead reckoning.

First, remember that wind and current may not merely retard your forward progress, but can also move you sideways if their directions and yours do not coincide. Gauging the effect of wind on your chosen course is largely a matter of past experience; when paddling in a side-wind in a *non*-dead-reckoning situation, file in your mental database how strongly it tends to push you, given your paddling skill and power.

With current, you have the advantage of charts and tables, the latter giving the current's predicted speed at a given point in time. If you are crossing a current (as opposed to either riding with it or bucking against it), the tables and your experience can give you an idea of how strongly and how far it might push you off-course.

The second factor is declination. Your compass's needle is attracted to the *magnetic North Pole*, the spot where the earth's magnetic pull is vertically downward. This point is nearly 1,000 miles from the *geographic North Pole*, the top of the "spindle" on which our planet spins.

Declination is the difference between the two, and in northern

Unless you have many years of experience at sea, dead reckoning should only be attempted when you have other navigational options at hand. For the inexperienced, a featureless expanse of water soon becomes confusing and even threatening.

Pacific waters off our continent it can be greater than 20 degrees. Marine charts treat this discrepancy through the compass rose, a graphical circle that looks much like the compass on your boat.

The compass rose solves your problem, but only if you remember to use it correctly. If it shows a declination of 20 degrees west and your desired heading is due south (180 degrees on your boat's compass), the actual heading you follow will be 200 degrees. Don't let fatigue or the disorientation of fog confuse you into forgetting to make this correction.

SHORE FEATURES AND RANGING

An onshore reference point that is unique, unsubmergible by tide, and well fixed — a lighthouse, say, or a large neon sign reading "EAT AT JOE'S" — provides a handy target, whether you are heading for the beach or merely looking to find your way around the point where it is located. Think of this as point-and-shoot navigation: As long as your bow is fixed on the shore feature — and it is growing visually larger — you are heading toward it.

Ranging, or transitting, is similar, but more sophisticated and informative. To range, you'll need a second shore feature between you and your target, positioned so you can line the two up, much as a rifler uses open sights. If the two objects diverge side-to-side from your point of view, you are

veering off-course. As a bonus, transitting provides an additional indicator of progress: When the near object appears to move closer to the far one, you are going forward; if this isn't happening, you definitely need to be paddling harder.

S A F E T Y

Prudent and secure boating always begins with precaution, whether you are piloting a kayak or a petroleum tanker. Appropriate clothing for the temperature of both water and air; necessary gear in good repair; a realistic assessment of your own abilities, along with confidence but not rashness; and knowledge through charts, guidebooks, and inquiry — all of these are mandates that when followed label you as an informed, competent kayaker whose heed of the basics protects the safety of yourself *and* your companions.

Besides the steps you'll take to deal with wind, waves, tide, and currents, two other on-water eventualities deserve your thoughtful consider-

ation. After that, you'll wish to add some safety gear to your ensemble.

UNPLEASANT SURPRISES

Both nature and other humans can interrupt the serenity of your tour through unexpected appearances. By anticipating them, you can avoid any untoward consequences.

Lightning

Because you have your strokes and boat savvy down, surface and below-surface hazards, real or potential, are less of a concern. So don't forget to look upward.

Lightning is not a force to toy with. The chances of being struck are

DID YOU KNOW

For the math freaks in the audience, could we have some specifics on the odds of being struck by lightning?

Actually, you'd think they would definitely not be in your favor, since on the average day, the earth experiences eight million lightning flashes.

However, over the course of a year, only about 400 people in the U.S. are hit by a bolt from the blue, and two-thirds survive the experience. The chance that you'll be struck is one in 625,000.

But then there is the case of Roy Sullivan, a park ranger in Virginia. Sullivan was first struck in 1942, and lost a big toenail. Twenty-seven years passed uneventfully — and then Sullivan was hit again in 1969 (singed eyebrows), 1970 (charred shoulder), 1972 (hair set aflame), 1973 (hair again), 1976 (ankle injury), and 1977 (torso burns). The human lightning rod died by his own hand in 1983, apparently after being rejected by a woman he was courting.

small — but make them even smaller. The head of a kayaker in open water is no more than 3 feet above the water's surface — but that makes you the highest point for some distance around, and lightning likes high contact points. Know the local forecast and the predictive day-to-day odds of a late-afternoon storm, and, if those odds are high, plan your trip to bring you to shore before the phenomenon strikes, or avoid going out in the first place.

If you choose to take the odds, keep a weather eye out, and don't venture farther than the point where you'll have time to beat the weather to shore. When a summer thundershower front approaches, abort your mission immediately.

Other Boats

Remember Mom's admonition when you were a tot: Don't play in traffic.

If you've discovered a secret kayaking spot so isolated that the only other denizens are piscine, good for you. I'd sure like to know where it is, but I don't expect you to tell me.

Otherwise, you'll be sharing the water with other craft. Those that should concern you are bigger (sometimes *way* bigger), faster (propelled by horsepower not person-power), and unfortunately sometimes not aware of your presence.

Assume they won't be on the lookout for you, and be on the lookout for them. On the ocean, you're most likely to encounter motorized vessels in shipping channels and near ports, large and small. When lake-touring, pay special attention to boats towing waterskiers. Their occupants have twice as much on their mind as those on other crafts: where they are going, and what's happening to their skier.

As you paddle your own boat, it's easy to fall into the trap of vague disdain for your high-powered colleagues. It's pointless. Most boaters, whatever their craft, are conscientious citizens of the water. They would no more deliberately pass perilously close to you than you would cut across a bank-fishing angler. It usually takes two to cause an accident; be generous rather than superior, and go out of your way to share the waterway.

Paddling toward the Seattle skyline, an admittedly extreme case of kayaks sharing a busy harbor with much larger vessels.

SAFETY EQUIPMENT

It's axiomatic that in any outdoor pursuit prevention overcomes possibility. Take, for example, an overnight backpacking trek when the weather forecast indicates a zero percent probability of precipitation. As long as you are toting along your waterproof shell, the sun will shine all day and stars will speckle the cloudless night sky. But leave it in the closet, and, sure as dawn, you'll be caught in a deluge of biblical proportions. This occurs so reliably that you are tempted to give up hiking and hire out as a rainmaker.

The identical principle applies to kayak safety: Carry preventives and you will never need them.

All right, so this is superstitious, and like any superstition should be taken with a grain of salt. But maybe — just maybe — there are a few items that might come in handy in a pinch.

The most skilled navigator can become temporarily lost or at peril through no fault of his own. A sudden mist or fog is disorienting; a sudden mist or fog out of which comes the sound of an ocean liner bearing down on you is downright dangerous.

A companion stops to work his pump without informing you, and when you look back he is nowhere in sight. Or you get in trouble — perhaps even flip — while lollygagging at your party's rear; when you surface your mates are several hundred yards ahead and blithely proceeding, unaware of your plight.

Some safety gear is optional, but what you choose to carry should be dictated by conditions. If they are variable or unpredictable, err on the side of caution. You won't pack a drysuit for a cruise in tropical water, but you might throw in a sunhat even when the forecast calls for cloudy skies.

Audible and Visual Signaling Devices

The human aural system, because it is stereoscopic, is an impressively effective directional device. Note how when you wish to home in on the source of a sound, you instinctively cock your head. Even though the sound reaches one ear only $1/5,000^{th}$ more quickly than the other, you can home in on it. This Doppler effect allows you to locate a

---

TECHNIQUE TIP

JIMINY CRICKET MEETS THE WEATHER CHANNEL

Q: If I'm sitting on the bank, shivering my butt off, and wondering whether to relaunch, can I really determine the temperature from a cricket's chirps?
A: You sure can, if you are privy to the secret formula: Count chirps per minute, subtract 40, divide by four, and add 50.

Here are a few other handy folkloric forecasting tips that really work.

● Note wind shifts, especially from north to south. "A wind from the south brings rain in its mouth."

● Other signs of an imminent storm: Mosquitoes and blackflies stop biting, milkweed pods fold up, and the frogs sound louder, because the increased humidity permits them to emerge from the water.

● The temperature is below 51 degrees if dandelions' petals close, and below 45 if you can see your breath.

companion when he hollers, "Hey, I'm over here!"

But if he is out of earshot, you'll both be better served by a signal sound that is sharper, more attenuated, and more abrupt in its onset. Under most conditions a whistle will do the job; eschew the inexpensive toy type for one sold by marine shops, with a lanyard for wearing it as a necklace.

A self-contained Klaxon, operated by compressed air or battery, provides a louder and more sustained blast. Your horn must be both operable when wet and accessible. If the horn you prefer does not have a flange extending from the bottom with a tie-hole punched in it, invest in a half foot of rubberized hose of a diameter that will slip snugly around the horn's shaft. Pinch the end of the hose together and secure with tape or glue, punch a hole in your jerry-rigged flange, and tie onto a line, either top-side or below your skirt.

Visual signals — and "water-proof" remains the watchword — range from a flashlight to a flare, hand-held or gun-launched. A flashlight is not only more familiar but easily deployed, though it does not have the flare's range. Make sure you choose a sealed model.

The flare is your signal of choice when a large motorized vessel has failed to take note of your presence, but it's more complex in its deployment and dangerous if used carelessly. Some flares involve burning phosphorus at very high temperatures — high enough to do nasty things to human skin. Ignite one under controlled conditions to get its feel, and treat a flare gun like any other weapon to be kept away from children. Off-water, store it unloaded, and on-water, watch your aim.

First Aid

The first aid kit is the apotheosis of gear you will never need — except when you need it.

Aspirin, antihistamine, and antacids are effective treatments for most of the general discomforts you might encounter on a trip. If the affliction is less ordinary — a fracture — the first rule is to get the patient to professional treatment as quickly as possible.

Otherwise, treat the condition or illness as conservatively as you can, and send for help. As with navigation, partial knowledge is likely to have a worse result than genuine knowledge.

A ready-made first aid
kit and specially
marked dry bag to
keep it in are sound
investments.

Use common
sense: Address
alleviation, and
leave treatment
to the pros.

Fortunately,
most in-field
medical situa-
tions will be
minor.
Splinters
and
head-
aches are
more likely
than fractures.

You can put
together a first aid kit of
your own, but it's easier and
only slightly more expensive to
purchase an assembled kit. A mid-
priced model designed for non-extreme
boating might typically include the following items:

- First aid manual
- Ace bandage
- Sterile bandages, compresses,
gauze, moleskin, butterfly closures,
and burn patches
- Medications for pain, nausea, consti-
pation, diarrhea, and bacterial infection
- Tape
- Tweezers and scissors
- Thermometer

A kit of this type costs about $50
and adds around 2 pounds to your gear
weight.

RESCUES

The first rule of kayaking is:
Any boat in any water can
flip.

Even if you have no intention of ever venturing beyond
pure glassy expanses, you
should know how to rescue
yourself, and how to assist
your partner's rescue — and
not only in theory. Hie
yourself and your
boat to the
warm pro-
tected water of a
pond or pool, and
dump as many times
as necessary to feel
that you've got it down.

Self-Rescue

You may never have to perform a
self-rescue, because as a prudent
boater you will seldom be out alone.
Still, you can get separated, lost, or —
we are all human — imprudent.
Knowing you can self-rescue and
never doing so is superior to its con-
verse.

THE PADDLE FLOAT. The key to self-
rescue is the paddle float, which fits
over one of your blades. They come in
inflatable and solid-foam models.
Inflatables are more compact when
deflated — but, of course, they aren't
much use in that state. In frigid water
when seconds matter, you must go
through several steps: getting hold of
the float (and you may have to remove
your gloves), blowing it up, and pulling

Self-Rescue with Paddle Float. 1) Pull yourself up and reach down to grab the coaming, then fall backwards, so your weight rights the kayak. 2) Secure one blade of the paddle under the the rear deck lines, then slip the paddle float over the other blade. 3) Facing the kayak, throw one leg over the paddle shaft. 4) Shinny to the boat and toward a prone position on the rear deck. 5) Keeping some of your weight on the paddle, insert both legs into the cockpit. 6) Flip your body and slide into the cockpit. Remove the float, stow it in its place, and pump water from your kayak.

it over the blade. Worse, a fumbled deflated bag can sink.

Foam takes up more cargo space, but it will always float, and its rigidity makes it easy to slip into place. Whichever your choice, the float should be readily available; under the rear deck lines is best.

The role of the paddle float is to turn your paddle into an outrigger support — a self-sustaining low brace — upon which you can climb back into the kayak.

When practicing the self-rescue under controlled conditions, bear in mind that, like an Eskimo roll, this is a technical exercise. Break it down into its steps, and practice to the point where those steps progress mechanically.

Paddle Float

Assisted Rescue

You'll wish to be as competent as a rescuing assistant as you are as a rescuee. Empathy always helps; remember that under the best of cir-

The only way you'll be able to rely on your ability to get back into a kayak in deep water is to practice the maneuver over and over again. Resist the urge to avoid flipping your boat; the more you do so, the more confident you'll be when you really need to rescue yourself.

cumstances, your partner in the water is, if nothing else, teed off at finding himself there. Under less ideal conditions, your partner may also be disconcerted, uncomfortable, or courting hypothermia if he isn't out of the soup in jig time (see Chapter 13).

Even with the most experienced kayaker in need of rescue, it doesn't hurt for you, as the assistant, to talk

TECHNIQUE TIP

MAKE MINE DECAF

Q: If I plan to spend a lot of time in cold water, is there a medication I can add to my first aid kit that will relieve hypothermia?

A: Unfortunately, the answer is no, but on-going research suggests there may be a prophylaxis. In a Canadian experiment, a combination of caffeine, the decongestant ephedrine, and theophylline, an asthma drug, significantly delayed hypothermia's onset. For reasons still obscure, within 30 minutes of administration, the mixture kick-starts fat metabolism to increase body-heat production by 20 percent. Incidentally, several cups of strong coffee won't do the trick. Caffeine alone has no effect on the corpus' internal furnace.

him through the steps. If circumstances require a drill-sergeant tone, use it; at the moment, you are not concerned about hurting his feelings.

In warm water, you have the luxury of first emptying the boat. Working in concert, the two people — one upright, the other still in the water — use muscle and body English to push the capsized boat onto

Here is a slight variation on the cata-kayak rescue (below).

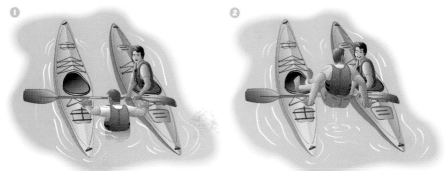

Cata-Kayak Rescue. 1) The rescuer "spoons" the two paddles together and braces them across both kayaks just behind the coaming. She presses down on the paddle shafts to help make the temporary cata-kayak a stable platform. 2) The swimmer places his hands on the rear decks, leans back and swings his feet over the paddle shafts. Pushing up, he levers himself into a seated position on the shafts, then slides back into his cockpit.

the foredeck of the other boat, and perpendicular to it. Once balanced in this position, a bit of end-to-end rocking will discharge the contents. After that, flip the boat over and slide it back into a floating configuration.

BACK INTO THE BOAT. Whatever maneuver gets you reseated is fine. In none will you appear as graceful as a gymnast, but klutzism is far less important than utility.

One method is to quick-rig a catamaran.

The Stirrup Rescue

Randel Washburne, in *The Coastal Kayaker's Manual* (see Sources & Resources), offers an alternative called the "stirrup rescue." It requires some setup and so is less suited to situations in which cold water or rough seas are a threat, but it provides significant stability.

The stirrup employs a rope about 15 feet long, tied into a loop. While using it, be certain to avoid entanglement.

Stability is terminated once the victim's weight is off the stirrup, so he should be prepared to complete the move as gracefully and expediently as possible. The rescuer can help by holding on to the victim's boat and pressing down hard with his own paddle to maintain the cross-boat catamaran.

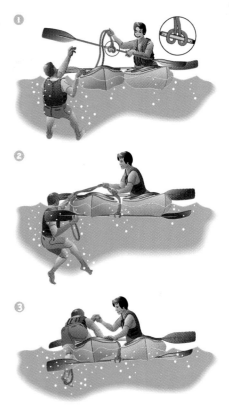

Stirrup-Sling Rescue. 1) Attach a loop of rope to one paddle shaft by threading it through itself (see detail). 2) The swimmer places the roped paddle under the two kayaks, while the rescuer braces them by laying the other paddle across the rear decks behind the coaming. 3) The swimmer places one foot in the secure loop and climbs into the cockpit. While he does so, the rescuer maintains downward pressure on the topside of the paddle to insure the platform's stability.

THE THRILL OF THE RIVER

In 1911, Caroline Lockhart negotiated Idaho's River of No Return as a passenger in a sweep barge, a 37-foot-long wooden craft propelled and steered by a massive single oar at the rear. The next year she wrote a compelling account of her voyage, which includes this vivid description of the rapid considered to this day the most hellacious on the river:

> Words seem inadequate and colorless when I think of describing the Big Mallard. As we stood among the boulders, looking at it in nothing less than awe, I could well understand the dread it inspired even [in experienced boatmen].
>
> The river, running like a mill race, came straight but comparatively smooth until it reached a high, sharp ledge of rock where the river made a turn. Then it made a close swirl and the current gave a sudden rush and piled up between two great rocks, one of which it covered thinly. Behind this latter rock the water dropped into a hollow that was like a well and when it rose it struck another rock immediately below that churned it into fury….
>
> No one spoke as we returned to the boats. My feet dragged and I had a curious goneness in the region of my belt buckle…. I lost faith in my life preserver, past

achievements in the water were no consolation....

It was in this frame of mind that I crawled limply into the boat.

♫

DID YOU KNOW

Like many rivers, especially in the mountainous West, the Salmon features several hot springs, where early-day boaters have built small pools for soothing streamside bathing. However, the springs are of a different order of magnitude in the town of Thermopolis on the Wind River in Wyoming, home to the largest hydrothermic site in the world. Here 18,600,000 gallons of 135 degree water are emitted daily, leaving a lamina of travertine, a calcium carbonate, that accumulates at a rate of five inches per decade. Even if you are not boating, Thermopolis (a few hours from Yellowstone National Park) offers kids and adults alike four pools fed by the springs, several water slides, a buffalo herd, and one of the finest small-town historical museums in the West. For an information packet, write Hot Springs State Park, 220 Park Street, Thermopolis, WY 82443, or call Park headquarters at 307-864-2176.

Eighty years later we perched on the cliff above Big Mallard, at a vantage that must have been close to where Caroline Lockhart and her companions scouted. There were twenty of us in the party, sixteen in rafts and myself and three others in whitewater slalom kayaks. We knew from *River of No Return*, the fine anecdotal guidebook by Johnny Carey and Cort Conley, of Lockhart's description. She had not exaggerated.

There was no question of the correct line; nearly all of the river's volume went left of the huge rock. And while the water on the other side was more gentle, we could see that it would push us inexorably toward the formation that Lockhart called "a well." In fact, it was a keeper hole as violent as any of us had ever seen in our combined half-century of kayaking. Like Lockhart, we recognized that the hole might be the superior of our PFDs.

We spent two hours atop that cliff, studying Big Mallard with a combination of trepidation and admiration. As both the kayakers and the trip leaders, we had some decisions to make. We were under no compulsion to run this Class IV+ rapid; across the river was a beach offering an easy portage. On the other hand, the challenge of Mallard was seductive.

We spoke in muted voices, and chose finally to send the rafts through.

Whitewater competitor Mary Hayes getting some thrills at the annual Ocoee Rodeo, a premier playboat event on the Ocoee River in Tennessee. Note that Mary is wearing a nose clip.

A helmet is required equipment for all whitewater kayakers, as is a PFD (personal flotation device). Note that this kayaker has a carabiner clipped to his shoulder, a useful device for assisted rescues.

Our boatmates were experienced and skilled, and unanimously wished to take a shot at it. In addition, the bigger and heavier rafts were less susceptible — though hardly immune — to the hole's grab.

The kayaks were another matter. A miscalculation that took one of the small boats too close to the rock would put it into the hole. The discussion continued.

One of the kayakers descended from the cliff, ferried across the river, and chose the portage. He reboarded and set up downstream as the safety boat.

The rafts set up and took aim. The first two passed the rock and went over the 6-foot drop on a perfect line, climbed the standing wave at the drop's bottom, and pushed over into the runout (the relatively flatwater after the wave). The third, however, got sideways just as it reached the boulder. For a moment that stopped the hearts of observers, the hole's edge tugged at its stern. Its paddlers threw their weight downstream and the raft snapped free.

Sometimes running a rapid like Big Mallard is an attenuated experience. Time slows; you remember every nuance, every stroke, every brace, every touch of the water on your boat. Afterward you can replay the run like a video set on slo-mo.

My shot through Mallard was the opposite; rather than a cohesive movie, it was selected short subjects: I recall the vee (see Chapter 12) between the rock and the cliffside, and knowing that I was hitting it with true aim. Flash-forward: The drop has somehow already happened, and the hole is so close to the side of my kayak that I could thrust my paddle into it — and so deep I would not touch water. Now the standing wave is behind me, though the only confirmations that I actually punched through it are the fact that I am upright, and the water smearing my eyeglasses.

I am eddied-out next to a raft, with no memory of making the eddy turn. The other two kayakers who did the run appear like magic in the back-eddy.

Nobody has anything to say. After a time, someone giggles. Soon all twenty of us are together again, laughing like a pack of idiot hyenas.

It is perhaps unfair to suggest that the touring kayaker is to the white-water kayaker as the day-hiker is to the technical climber. But that won't stop the river-runner from making such comparisons.

The whitewater kayaker will also insist that the goal of a tourer is to get across water; the goal of a riverperson is to get into water. For pure frustration, volunteer to pilot the support raft;

TECHNIQUE TIP

HEADS UP!

Although the odds of an underwater head injury during a capsize are not great, accidents do happen. The lesson: You should always keep a watchful eye on fellow boaters when they do go into the drink.

Take, for example, the case of my friend Jake Turquist, an experienced and skillful kayaker. We were out on Montana's Big Blackfoot River some years ago when Jake had a routine capsize while wave-surfing. By sheer bad luck he struck a rock outcropping that caught him in the forehead a half inch below the brim of his helmet. Although he did suffer a concussion and a cut that required stitches, he made it out of the boat and was hauled in by the support raft.

Long odds aside, any time even the most seasoned kayaker flips in the most apparently benign circumstances, all other boaters within eyeshot should give him their full attention until he is upright, or signals he is okay — and should be prepared to go to his assistance if mishap occurs.

Incidentally, should you wish to search out the spot in which Turquist met the rock, ask any western Montana boater to show you. The word of the incident spread, and all now know the rapid as Turquist Falls.

Playboating on a serious hydraulic on the Lochsa River in the Selway-Bitterroot Wilderness in northern Idaho. Notice the liberal use of duct tape on the helmet.

you are likely to doze off repeatedly as you park in this back-eddy, while your skinny-boat rivermates take just one more shot at some surfing wave or ender hole.

Whitewater kayakers are "insiders"; they'd have you think that they are members of a secret society with its own rote and ritual. Each weekend morning they rendezvous at the truck stop closest to the put-in, scarfing down doughnuts and coffee as their mates arrive. On the river, they will perch at clifftop for what seems an endless time, debating the best line through the rapid below — not because they are concerned so much as because it's the thing to do.

THE WHITEWATER KAYAK

A whitewater kayak is a versatile tool for a variety of water. You can join your canoeist friends on a jaunt down a meandering Class I river, and take advantage of your streamline and efficiency to keep up with less effort than they must expend. Or you can leave them in your wake if you feel like working up a head of steam. Yet with intermediate skills, you can take on Class IV water that threatens to swamp a canoe paddled by experts, and enjoy playing in felicitous standing waves along the way. (For details on the Class I–VI ratings of river difficulty, see Chapter 12.)

While its round hull makes the whitewater boat more tippy than a touring kayak, the same design feature facilitates rolling up — and anyway, tippiness is in the mind-set of the kayaker. Your greater rocker offers maneuverability.

Similarly, the feeling that the smaller boat is more confining is illusory, or at best psychological; a well-fitted slalom kayak is as comfortable as its bigger touring relative, and a smaller boat feels — and is — more controllable. When your bow point is a mere 5 feet in front of you, turning it in the direction you want to go is easier.

Choosing Your Kayak

Because kayak design is a mature art, it is difficult to pick a craft that is simply lousy. With intermediate skills

and in intermediate water, you can select a boat almost at random with confidence it will get you through the rapids and respond to your roll.

But once you've had the chance to try a variety of kayaks, personal preferences, colored by your abilities and informed by the advice of an experienced outfitter, will direct you toward

Before you buy a kayak, try as many models as you can get your hands on. Swap with other kayakers on river outings to find the style boat that best suits you.

the right boat. Before you buy, rent kayaks or attend tryout "demo days" that many retailers stage in season; swap with other kayakers on river trips; and otherwise try as many models as you can.

In the course of this experimentation, note that length is the controlling factor in the size of a whitewater boat. The average contemporary boat is about 11 feet long, though it will vary, plus or minus, a foot or two. Begin with the longest, and work down from

Valley Falls, Tygart River, West Virginia. Rivers don't get much more thrilling than this. Running waterfalls is, of course, for the highly advanced kayaker only.

there. When you get to the kayak whose initial stability and directional stability are too great a challenge to your abilities, move back up to the next longest model.

Whitewater Equipment

The gear list for river-running is, in its most spare application, pared down to five items besides the boat: paddle, spray skirt, flotation, PFD, and helmet. The discussion of the first four in Chapter 2 applies equally to touring and whitewater.

The fifth item — the helmet — is not optional, unlike the case in touring. Most often, the river rapid that flips you is formed by a rock. If your

head meets it, bad things can happen.

Choose a helmet designed for the sport, and make certain it fits, for both effectiveness and comfort. Visored models are available, or add a banded stand-alone visor; the latter is also nice sun protection onshore.

INTERMEDIATE
TECHNIQUES

Kayakers come in different modes — and so does whitewater; both can be more or less aggressive. A stern rudder will turn your bow into that standing wave, but if it also serves to bring you to a halt halfway up the wave's face, you can soon expect to be moving backwards, and not necessarily in an upright position.

COMPOUND STROKES

You're ahead of the game when you combine two (or more) strokes and braces into a compound move that addresses the keys to negotiating whitewater: maintaining momentum and bracing. Sometimes, as when you are cutting into an eddy or surfing a backwave, the need for a brace can be anticipated, but often it is a reaction of the moment, and quickness counts. With your paddle in the water, you are ready to convert a stroke to a brace — or to execute a paddle move that is both — and you've got a jump on the river's whims. Combination strokes are like all-weather tires: They handle several conditions at once.

A set of handy compound strokes combine draws and pries with power strokes. They let you make course corrections, maintain momentum, and brace all at once, a useful maneuver when negotiating whitewater; depending on conditions, they can be quite subtle or fairly aggres-

The Draw-Power Stroke and the Pry-Power Stroke

These power strokes begin or end with draws and/or pries (reverse draws) to turn the boat. The difference between them is that the draw-power stroke either begins or ends with the draw depending on which way you want to turn; the pry-power stroke is a draw/stroke/pry or a pry/stroke/draw combination depending on which way you want to turn. (Among canoeists, these strokes are known as the J-stroke and C-stroke respectively, because those are the shapes they describe in the water when viewed from above.) Note that the power face of the paddle blade turns so it is following the stroke's path.

Eddy Turns and the Duffek

When, in the 1953 world Whitewater Slalom championships at Geneva, the Czech kayaker Milovan Duffek introduced the paddle move that now bears his name, it was considered revolutionary. Until then, the brace, draw, turning stroke, and forward stroke were members of a family; the Duffek weds them into one efficient entity.

The Duffek is the most elegant of compound paddle moves, combining several elements of stroking and bracing into a maneuver that is at the same time versatile, useful, and satisfyingly flashy.

A Typical Eddy (top). The main current is channeled past the protruding rock, then back-fills, resulting in an upstream flow behind the obstacle. The eddy line is the boundary between the main downstream flow and the eddy's upstream flow. Caught On an Eddy line (bottom). Unless he quickly employs braces and strokes, this kayaker risks being capsized either to the left or right, depending on whether the downstream or upstream flow is more powerful.

sive. In a sense, these simple strokes come naturally as you become comfortable with what you and your kayak can do on the water.

Eddies can be large enough to hold a dozen kayaks or they can be tiny pockets with room enough to shelter just one boat, as here on the Trinity River in northern California.

Because the Duffek is usually used for entering an eddy, let's jump the gun on Chapter 12, which treats whitewater morphology, and take a look at how and why an eddy works, and what it can do to a kayak.

When water flows past a constricting shoreline protuberance, its momentum wants to carry it on in a straight course. Gravity, on the other hand, requires that it fill in the void below the obstruction. To do so, the water flows back upstream once its momentum wanes.

This backflow is the eddy. If the river's slope is steep enough, and/or the obstruction is sufficiently sharp to significantly disrupt downriver current, the backflow forms an eddy line, a friction seam where water moves against itself. It's not unusual to see an eddy line so sheer that the water going in one direction is visibly several inches higher than the water going in the other direction.

As a kayak crosses an eddy line entering an eddy at the perpendicular, its bow is spun upstream, its stern downstream; exiting, its bow is spun downstream, its stern upstream. Since your countermeasures are the same — or more accurately, mirror images — entering or exiting an eddy, I'll choose for illustration "eddying out," or leaving the main current for the protection of an eddy.

The Duffek Turn. 1) The kayaker plants a high brace into the eddy line and begins to pivot on it. 2) As the bow enters the eddy, the brace becomes a draw stroke. 3) With the kayak farther into the eddy, the draw is turned into a power stroke.

You'll be doing so a lot. Eddies are the river's "rest stops," a place to catch your breath or from which to scout the rest of the rapid. If you are camping, or just stopping for lunch, eddies are fine harbors sheltered from the river's push. Eddies are also the river equivalent of the skier's rope tow: Often the best surfing wave or ender hole of a set of rapids is at the eddy's upstream end, and the backflow provides an effortless way to return to the hydraulic as many times as you like.

The duffek turn, the most elegant and effective of all compound strokes. Here the kayaker is just turning his high brace into a draw stroke.

But first you've got to cross the often-powerful eddy line.

To visualize the potential pitfall, consider a boat crossing an eddy line with no forward momentum. The backflow pushes its bow upstream; the channel flow pushes the stern downstream. Equilibrium is reached; the kayak is backwards to the river flow, directly on the eddy line.

You are upside down, unless you've got your braces down cold. The opposite flows that just spun you are now grappling at your sides. Tilt the slightest degree from horizontal trim, and the conflicting waters will be glad

effect on stability.

To visualize the superiority of the Duffek in crossing an eddy line, compare it to the high-brace turn. In both, your momentum is already up, thanks to hard paddling on your approach. With the high brace, as you hit the line you plant your paddle upstream and lean hard on it. You've established a temporary third point (after the bow and stern) and the opposing currents do the rest. As long as your speed was

Peeling Out of an Eddy. Perhaps counter to commonsense, the preferred way to leave an eddy is to aim upstream (top), toward the head of the eddy. The more momentum you have when you hit the eddy line the better. Then, as the main current catches your bow (bottom), the boat is turned downstream.

to grab your dipped edge and help you over the rest of the way.

Successfully eddying-out depends on three aspects of mechanics. First, the presentation of the kayak should be such that you cross at a right angle. Second, you are prepared to brace upstream. Third — and as always — you are paddling vigorously, to take advantage of momentum's positive

authoritative, the plant of your brace forms a pole on which you twirl, and you end up well shoreward of the line, pointing upstream.

In other words, the high brace does the job — but note how the Duffek does the job better.

The Duffek begins with the same high brace — and "high" is the operative term. Depending on the power of

Five kayakers confer in the relatively slack water of an eddy near a hole in the Payette River, southwestern Idaho.

Peeling Out. The kayaker hits the eddy with his bow pointing somewhat upstream in anticipation of the main current swinging him around. As it does, he plants a high brace on the downstream side, pivots on the brace, and turns the brace into a power stroke as his boat clears the eddy.

the eddy line, an 80-degree angle is not too great. A helpful technical device when you're practicing is to check, in more gentle, beginning eddy lines, whether your forearm is horizontal and a few inches higher than the top of your head; if so, your brace is assertive. Another way to confirm the correctness of this position is a flick of the eyes; if you are turned well into the Duffek, you should be able to catch sight of your stern.

As your bow crosses the line, turn the brace into a draw stroke angled toward it. Here the aspect to be remembered is that you are setting up for a driving stroke — *without* removing blade from water. Instead of fighting the spin factor, you are abetting it; your kayak is turning upstream even faster than the opposing currents can take it. All that remains is to get well clear of the eddy line; to do so, turn the draw into a stroke, and the next thing you know, you're bobbing in the eddy's forgiving bosom.

Like the Eskimo roll, the Duffek is technical but not difficult once you get it down, and becomes instinctual with practice. Try it first in a pool or on flatwater by picking a point representing an imaginary eddy line. Paddle hard toward it, and execute a Duffek. Once you are able to make a sharp turn of at least 90 degrees, proceed on to an actual eddy. Begin at its downstream end where the flow is perceivable but less powerful, and work your way upstream. With an hour or so of practice, you'll be snapping off Duffeks with the precision of a West Point cadet performing a salute. From here on, when you encounter eddy lines, your greatest problem will be maintaining modesty in the light of your comrades' admiration.

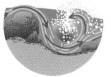

ON THE RIVER

12

Fifty yards of Class III rapids look chaotic at first glance, and as the term "chaos" is understood in contemporary physics, they are. As you become fluent in river reading, you'll learn that the behavior of water moving downhill is surprisingly predictable. Everything it does is a function of gravity and friction.

The latter is caused by one of four opposing forces against which the river moves: its bottom; objects, usually boulders and ledges, rising up from that bottom, to a point either above or below the surface; the shore; and other water, as in the case of the eddy, in which water below an obstruction in the river flows upstream.

WHITEWATER FORMATIONS

Before you fasten your spray skirt for a maiden voyage down the Hypothetical Fork of the Whitewater River, let's do some scouting. In its course, we'll discuss the varieties of waves, rapids, and other formations you can expect to find.

The Hypo (as the locals have dubbed the Hypothetical Fork) is a pool-and-drop river, always a good choice for a shakedown run. The drops, where the river loses elevation over a short distance, provide the fun stuff. The pools below them (more accurately, water that still moves downstream but at a lesser speed and without noticeable steepness) let the river take a breather, and so can you.

Hypothetical Fork of the Whitewater River

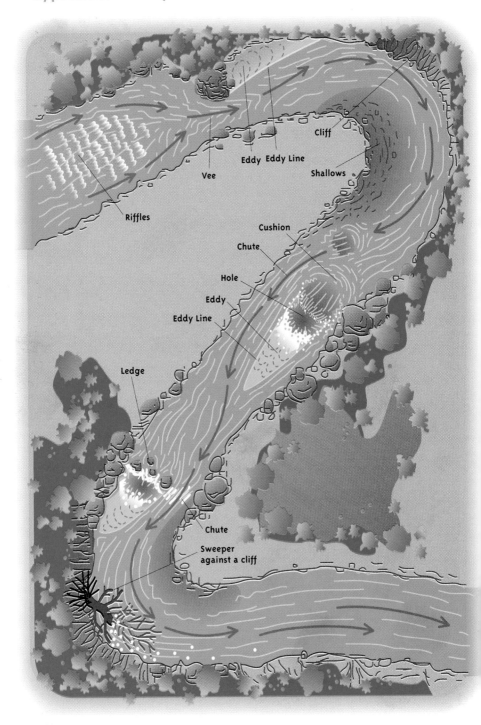

The stretch we are scouting is rated overall at Class III, meaning that it includes irregular waves, a significant drop, and features that might require complex maneuvering. Class III water is challenging but well within the abilities of an intermediate kayaker who is comfortable in the boat and confident in his basic strokes and braces, and in his Eskimo roll. (For more on river ratings, see pages 146-148.)

A vee formation, Fish Creek, Idaho. Experienced kayakers often prefer to aim to one side or the other on the vee, in this case to the left side, away from the boulder on the right.

Riffles

You approach toward a section that's wide and shallow; while you are still well upstream, you determine that the water isn't very deep by noting that its color up ahead becomes less aquamarine and more brown, reflecting the character of the bottom. It's more or less level gravel, creating a riffle, a set of innumerable standing waves at most 6 inches high, peaked but not white-capped. Bob through bow-on, or try turning sideways with a sweep and planting a downstream brace. It's good practice but probably unnecessary to keep you upright; hip action also will serve in this introductory Class I section.

Vees

After a runout (another term for the pool, or flatwater, after the riffle), the Hypo narrows. On the right are shallows, which dump most of the volume into the deeper channel, and on

A kayaker plays in a hole on the Piedra River in the San Juan Mountains of southern Colorado as two mates look on. This hole is the last drop on a Class IV stretch of the river known as the Mud Slide Rapid.

"face-washers." Here's the chance to use your compound strokes, the combinations that keep the boat both in trim and moving faster than the water for stability.

Many rapid sets are "sneakable": There is no rule that says you can't take a course a bit to either side of the waves' greatest height. You do, however, move closer to another old hydrodynamic friend, one who might have something in mind for you.

The Eddy

As you pass the rock on the left, you see the eddy behind it, along with the eddy line. In the same way that you've noticed that the standing waves diminish as you continue downstream, so does the power of the eddy line — and its ability to play tricks if you are sneaking and get grabbed. Your Duffek or high-brace eddy turn will carry you through, but they work best when you are dealing with the line because you have chosen to cross it, rather than having it catch you.

You do cross (or "eddy-out"), to congratulate yourself on running those waves and to boat-scout the next formation. You've already noted that the river bends fairly sharply after the next runout.

Bends

This bend skirts a cliff wall, providing a classic example of the effect of shore friction on river flow.

A river is like a rolling stone; not only does it gather no moss, but it wants to continue in the direction gravity is

the left a rock pushes the water toward the middle.

Color once again indicates where the shallows end and the channel begins, but with this slightly steeper drop you have another visual cue. The water coming off the shallows to one side and off the rock on the other pillows up in non-breaking swells which come together to form an inverted vee, a smooth pointed green tongue delineated by the swells' pillows. This is a gunsight showing where you want to aim.

Beyond the vee's point you hit the standing waves. These are sharp-faced, as much as a yard high, and curling toward you; you might encounter a few taking it. When a wall obstructs that direction, the river has no choice but to…well, go with the flow. Indeed, the river is responsible for that vertical wall; over geological eons, its pounding has carved the wall's shape.

The cliff does not stop at the waterline; it continues straight down, producing the deepest — and swiftest — part of the channel. It's not as daunting as it looks. The water is your ally; it wants to take you where it is going. The first time you navigate a bend, cheat a little away from the curve's elbow and toward the shallow; the eddy line on that side will be far less grabby. Simultaneously, note where the cliffside eddy line is and, for

Not all ledges are undercut like the one on the Hypothetical Fork. This one, on the Gauley River in West Virginia, is known as pillow rock. The water slamming into it bounces back off, forming a large pillow.

ducing the deepest — and swiftest — part of the channel. At the same time, as it hits the wall, some of the water is "rubbed off." Unlike the protruding rock you just passed, the cliff's effect is more abrupt and the water had no time to pillow into swells. Instead, you are likely to find powerful eddy lines.

Your line here is to stay in the future reference, how strongly it flows.

The key to the unobstructed bend (we'll treat obstructed bends in a moment) is that eddy line. As long as you don't engage it, that cliff will tower above you, but you'll glide blithely past.

Holes

Like eddies, holes result from obstruc-

Hole   Keeper Hole

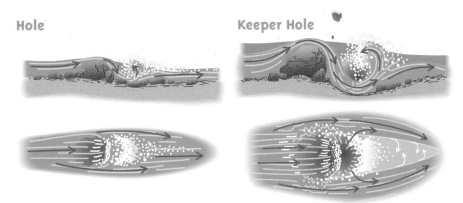

Left: The river bottom downstream from the rock is relatively shallow and the water volume is moderate. The result is a less pushy standing wave; you could probably punch through the wave with quick, vigorous power strokes. Right: Here the depression pounded out by high-volume water crashing down a significant drop makes for a keeper hole. Scout for such hydraulics, and give them a wide berth.

tions, almost always rocks. In the case of the hole, the upper part of the rock can be above water, or it may be submerged a few inches. Whichever, upstream of the rock the water is channeled to either side, and downstream the rock creates a vacuum into which some of that water must dump.

Aside from water volume and velocity, a hole's power is a function of the rock's size, shape, and how deeply the rock is submerged — or not sub-

merged. In the most benign case, an underwater rock that has been worn smooth by eons of erosion will create a pillow, not a hole. Pillows are similar to ocean swells in their action: A rock well below the surface forces the water to bulge up as it passes over, no hole results, and you can ride the bulge in safety.

If the rock is more jagged and closer to the surface, the river is likely to break over it. On the downstream

TECHNIQUE TIP

NO, PLEASE, AFTER YOU

One effective way to judge the height of a drop is to get one of your pals to run it before you. Peeling into an eddy above and mumbling something on the order of "I need to check my spray skirt" is a good tactic. Then watch to see how far past the drop the other boater goes before she reappears. If, when she does, she's bottom-side up, that's additionally informative.

But seriously, don't be afraid to admit it when you're feeling a little shaky about a stretch of water. Just ask a more experienced kayaker to run the rapids first so you can see the right line to take.

The hydraulic below the Great Falls of the Potomac is unquestionably a potential keeper, although highly experienced kaykers successfully run the falls regularly.

side, the water plunges; if it does so with enough power, the hole will be visible as an actual depression.

In an attempt to fill in this depression, water returns upstream — but again there must be a counterbalance, or the hole would overflow, incidentally defying gravity's laws. The water does this by escaping at depth and buoying back up — where, if the hydraulic is radical, it will fall again into the hole.

If the hole is sufficiently powerful, it becomes a "keeper" — and if you are out of the boat, you are the kept. The hole brings you up — and then drags you right back down. This becomes tedious after a while (not to mention dangerous). Luckily, the situation is usually avoidable and almost always escapable with the right technique (see page 162).

When, as in this stretch of the Hypo, a Volkswagen-sized rock is above water and the river drops visibly to either side from your upstream vantage, you can safely assume a hole behind it. But holes resulting from submerged boulders can be equally powerful, and are best given a miss. Look for two significant pillows in steep water, with whitecapped waves downstream. You might see the swirl of a back-eddy beyond the drop. Execute a sweep stroke or a rudder and skim past to one side, glancing over to see what you have missed.

Hitting an exposed rock is jarring,

builds up, forming cushions, or pillows. These bulges are often enough to nudge you to one side or the other.

Another reason you won't hit the rock is that you've set up well in advance, choosing the channel to the right with most of the volume. As you get closer — and build up momentum — you spot the mini-vee. You shoot through it with authority, the same authority you apply to all of your moves in the next 10 seconds.

Rodeo champ Chris Spelius in the midst of performing a pirouette in a surf hole on the Ocoee River, Tennessee.

and broaching against it is perilous to kayak and kayaker (see page 161). Luckily, with a rock the size of this one in the Hypo, it's virtually impossible to do. Remembering that water wants to flow in a straightforward line, note how it must be thwarted from this goal as it slams into the boulder — it has to go around. Before it can, it

The greater the drop, the more powerful the keeper hole to the side, and the taller and steeper the standing wave into which you are punching. At this moment, you are in a *reverse*, a hydrodynamic or a combination of hydrodynamics that wants to claw you to a stop and then have its way with you.

If your stern strays into the eddy line or beyond, the hole jerks at it. Simultaneously, if you don't have the speed to climb and punch the crest of that first standing wave, it will toss you to the hole like a bone to a dog.

The authority you use to maintain forward progress is not only a matter of powerful strokes, but also of a forward or sideways lean aggressive enough to reach somewhere to put those strokes. An "air brace" is comical to the shore-side observer, but no laughing matter to you at the moment. As you crest that first wave, your hull-water interface is minimal, and a lot of the water is far below. What water there is will be unusually aerated, and, as a support medium, air is for airplanes. The solution is to bring yourself to the water, with whatever angle of lean does the chore. The firm stroke-and-brace you'll then perform will propel you to the next, and smaller, wave.

Once past the rock and its hole, take a closer look at what you've just successfully negotiated. The water has been pushed to either side; now it wants to get back to the middle. The outside edges of the two channels are falling inward — a lot of the outside edges, and with a lot of power.

Playing

Flash-forward to your next run of the Hypo. Having eyeballed the water below the rock, you've noted an attractive "play wave," and this time you decide to give it a go.

As you drop past the rock, you turn left and cross the eddy line with a smart Duffek. You are suddenly facing upstream — and no longer moving. The feeling is eerie: The river races

TECHNIQUE TIP

ROLL MODELS

Rolling after a capsize in whitewater can be more difficult than in a swimming pool, especially if you are in a hole or the surface above you is so turbulent that it provides less purchase (greater aeration) for your sweep. But, more often, your concern will be remaining upright once you get there.

The fact that a roll naturally ends in a high brace is a major assist, but only if combined with knowing how your boat is oriented when you have that brace. Your first piece of business when you come up is to observe where you are in relation to the current and its effects. As soon as you do, you are back in paddling mode: bracing downstream if you are sideways, power-stroking in the same direction if that is where you are facing, or sweeping around to surf or endo once again, if you are determined that this hydraulic has met its match in you.

Post-roll whitewater recovery is discussed in Chapter 13.

past on either side in huge mounding haystacks, but in your pocket of harbor you are stable and motionless on flat-water.

In front of your bow, between you and the hole, is a standing wave of a different sort. Caused by the water the hole kicks out, it's built sort of back-wards: Its break is downstream, while its upstream face is gently sloped. The main turbulence is the wave's trough, where it edges into the hole.

This is, in microcosm, the perfect play formation, for surfing and enders.

Surfing

To surf the wave, edge forward and up onto it (the eddy, if it is moving at all, will be taking you in this direction anyway). At the right equilibrium, you'll be static in relation to the bank. You *won't* be sideways static, however; as the wave surges, much squirrelli-ness will be torquing at you. Set the paddle low, and be ready for frequent quick braces and mini-strokes to keep you upright and trimmed.

Enders

A power stroke or two can, on certain waves, drive you from Surf City to Enderville. The ender, or "endo," is the nearest move to free flight a kayak can perform, and a thing of beauty and exhilaration. A few years ago in western Montana, one kayaker, after an endo that launched him like a rocket, exclaimed, with reference to the brain chemicals usually lumped under the heading "adrenaline," "Why do you think they call them 'endo'-morphins?"

This hole on the Hypo, you've learned by checking in advance with fellow kayakers more familiar than you with the river, is powerful enough for endo-ing, but not so strong that you won't be able to get free of the hole if you find yourself in the drink (see page 162). You deliberately allow the hole to suck in your bow, the deeper the better, and the combined buoyancy of you and your boat allows you to be taken in, but only to a point. Eventu-ally, what goes up must come down — or vice versa in this case. As if you tasted bad, the hole spits you out — like a cannon spits a cannonball. Depending on your approach angle, you may shoot straight up into the air.

Endo-ing is the paradigm of pushing beyond the envelope, and you should expect to capsize frequently. If your roll is sufficiently solid, this won't faze you; if not, stay out of holes.

Ledges

A ledge is an obstruction that runs perpendicular across the river. The one on this stretch of the Hypo leaves a gap to the right, and unless you like to live dangerously, you'll take it rather than going "over the falls" — although you may choose to eddy-out below the ledge and do some more playing.

Ledges that stretch uniformly from bank to bank are often the work of humans, usually in the form of dams. Such ledges, whatever their ori-gins, are to be taken seriously, scouted assiduously, and portaged if there is the outside possibility of danger.

At the bottom of any dam swirls a reversal of some kind. Not only can it be as powerful as a hole, but it is uniform across the breadth of the river, without passages through which you can maneuver. This reversal not only can "keep" you but can also slam you against the dam's wall. Worse, you may not be the only one "kept"; this sort of reversal is fond of retaining logs, flotsam, and miscellaneous debris. Tangling — literally — with this kind of obstruction is way beyond going outside the envelope. It doesn't even have your return address on it.

Sweepers

Also called "strainers," these insidious obstacles above and below the surface form a barrier to your progress. It's easy to hypothesize how the multi-branched tree got stuck at this point along the Hypo.

Before you set out on today's trip, high spring runoff compromised its root-hold and ripped it from its tenuous bankside mooring. After a trip of its own, it hung up when it caught on a rock, say, or was left partially high and dry by a drop in water level. Now it is rotting away in the elbow of this river-bend to the left.

In its way, the tree naturally gravitated toward the main flow of the current, so in the current is where it stopped — directly in the path of where the river wants to take you.

Sweepers are to be avoided at all costs. I discuss the power and weight of moving water in more detail in Chapter 13, but already on this trip

Kayak champ Bob McDonough in the midst of an endo, Ocoee River, Tennessee. The Ocoee is a Mecca for playboaters across the country.

you've had a solid introduction to the phenomenon. You can also see how a boat that hits a sweeper will be swept sideways against it, and might well be pinned beneath in an upside-down position. You'll probably be able to get out of the boat; whether you'll be able to get out from under the sweeper is another question.

Since the sweeper is in the current of the sort of sharp bend you previously boated, you know that chances are that the bank on the inside crux of the elbow is gently sloped. If you have any question about your ability to paddle well clear, take advantage of this forgiving bank and portage.

But you may reasonably judge this sweeper as doable. If so, set up to the right and well in advance, noting the location of the eddy line and snuggling up as closely as possible without entering. Here the current is slowest and most forgiving, but the greater flow will try to pull you across the river

toward the hazard. Be ready to ferry, just as you would in an ocean current (see Chapter 7). With the bow angled away from the tree, ease on downstream at your own pace; once past, let the current swing you around and back into the main channel.

GAUGING THE RIVER

The effects of shore configuration, midstream rocks, and the like on a river's morphology are further determined by gradient, velocity, and volume. No single one will tell you exactly how the river will behave, but evaluated in a holistic way, they can provide valuable indicators.

Gradient

A watercourse's steepness has everything to do with the sited features. A

TECHNIQUE TIP

CHANGING THE CHANNEL

As the early spring runoff gives way to lower river volume, submerged gravel bars may emerge as longitudinal islands, presenting a choice of channels to either side. When there is an evident difference in volume, take the channel with the greater flow.

Otherwise, choose the channel that drops at the island's upstream end, by looking for a more pronounced vee followed by standing waves, however small. The other channel may well be higher owing to some obstruction at the other end, most probably shallows. Even given your kayak's low draft, bottom-scraping — or even the embarrassment of having to get out and walk — is a distinct possibility.

?

DID YOU KNOW

The first descent of the Colorado River through the Grand Canyon, by John Wesley Powell and eight other men in 1869, is all the more impressive by several factors: Hardly a day passed without at least one of his party taking a nerve-shattering swim; provisions became soaked and spoiled; 115-degree days were followed by rain-soaked nights; and Powell had only one arm.

On August 28, as Powell's group bivouacked above a daunting set of rocks, holes, and rollers, Billy Dunn and the brothers O.G. and Seneca Howland decided they'd had a bellyful. They'd discovered a trail out of the Canyon, and the next morning they took it. Powell wished them luck, and hit the river. Within hours, Powell found flatwater, and the next day he exited the Canyon at Grand Wash Cliffs.

Dunn and the Howlands, meanwhile, were crossing the desert, unknowingly within a few miles of three prospectors who had molested a Shivwits Indian woman. That night, a tribal posse avenged the insult by murdering the three men in their sleep in a tragic case of mistaken identity.

mile-wide meandering flatland river in which a line of yard-apart boulders crops up presents one navigational challenge; a 40-foot waterfall crashing down on the same line is another kettle of fish — or, if you're not careful, fish food.

Gradient is the ratio of vertical drop to horizontal distance. As with all of a river's vital statistics, it is merely a rough guide to ferocity, informative only when other measurements are factored in. A river that falls 300 feet per mile is guaranteed to include thrills and chills. But so might a river rated at 20 feet per mile, if that 20 feet consists of a five-foot waterfall every 400 yards or so. Yet another river with the same overall gradient might be so evenly sloped as to be a hard-paddling slog. In that case, if you are seeking whitewater adventure, you've come to the wrong place.

Velocity

Remember the effects of friction and impact? It's easy to visualize that faster-moving water will produce greater friction, and smash off impediments with more violence and heightened turbulence-induced effects.

Open your bathtub tap to a trickle. The flow makes barely a splash before running down the drain. Now imagine that the Hypo Fork is dam-controlled, and upstream they've shut off most of the water. That keeper hole behind Volkswagen Rock is a pussycat, because the river is moving so slowly it can take its time easing on downstream, without detouring into the pit.

If you are paying attention, you'll see a flaw in this reasoning, though. Velocity is only one indicator of a river's force, and it cannot be considered in isolation.

Volume

As Albert Einstein demonstrated, energy is the product of mass and velocity. The lower the mass of water, the lower the river's speed. In other words, velocity — and its effects — is inextricably tied to the amount of water that is moving.

Gauging volume is not appreciably

The velocity and volume of a river are highly variable from month to month, and can greatly affect the severity of its rapids. During spring high water, this falls produces a major hydraulic.

more sophisticated than the way you addressed the issue when you were a kid asking, "I wonder how deep that creek is?" You jabbed a stick into it. The major refinement is that the gauge is marked in feet and permanently installed at a particular point along the river's flow, and from the level that the water reaches on it, assumptions can be made as to the effect of volume on downstream hydraulics.

Especially on a river that is fed by snowmelt, volume can increase and decrease radically over the course of a season; the same is true of the volume on a given day in one year compared to

THE INTERNATIONAL SCALE OF RIVER DIFFICULTY

Class ratings of a given river's challenge have been codified by the American Whitewater Affiliation, an organization that promotes whitewater adventuring in all appropriate crafts.

This is the American version of a rating system used to compare river difficulty throughout the world. This system is not exact; rivers do not always fit easily into one category, and regional or individual interpretations may cause misunderstandings. It is no substitute for a guidebook or accurate firsthand descriptions of a run.

Paddlers attempting difficult runs in an unfamiliar area should act cautiously until they get a feel for the way the scale is interpreted locally. River difficulty may change each year due to fluctuations in water level, downed trees, geological disturbances, or bad weather. Stay alert for unexpected problems.

As river difficulty increases, the danger to swimming paddlers becomes more severe. As rapids become longer and more continuous, the challenge increases. There is a difference between running an occasional Class IV rapid and dealing with an entire river of this category. Allow an extra margin of safety between skills and river ratings when the water is cold or if the river itself is remote and inaccessible.

CLASS I: Easy. Fast moving water with riffles and small waves. Few obstructions, all obvious and easily missed with little training. Risk to swimmers is slight; self-rescue is easy.

CLASS I

CLASS II

CLASS II: Novice. Straightforward rapids with wide, clear channels which are evident without scouting. Occasional maneuvering may be required, but rocks and medium-sized waves are easily missed by trained paddlers. Swimmers are seldom injured and group assistance, while helpful, is seldom needed.

CLASS III: Intermediate. Rapids with moderate, irregular waves which may be difficult to avoid and which can swamp an open canoe. Complex maneuvers in fast current and good boat control in tight passages or around ledges are often required; large waves or strainers may be present but are easily avoided. Strong eddies and powerful current effects can be found, particularly on large-volume rivers. Scouting is advisable for inexperienced parties. Injuries while swimming are rare; self-rescue is usually easy but group assistance may be required to avoid long swims.

CLASS IV: Advanced. Intense, powerful but predictable rapids requiring precise boat handling in turbulent water. Depending on the character of the river, it may feature large, unavoidable waves and holes or constricted passages demanding fast maneuvers under pressure. A fast, reliable eddy turn may be needed to initiate maneuvers, scout rapids, or rest. Rapids may require "must" moves above dangerous hazards. Scouting is necessary the first time down. Risk of injury to swimmers is moderate to high, and water conditions may make self-rescue difficult. Group assistance for rescue is often essential but requires practiced skills. A strong

continued on page 148

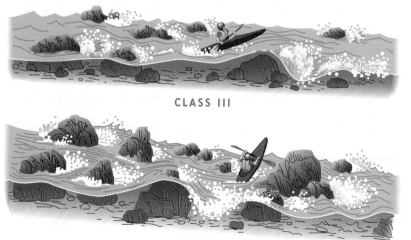

CLASS III

CLASS IV

CLASS V

RIVER DIFFICULTY
continued from page 147

Eskimo roll is highly recommended. CLASS V: Expert. Extremely long, obstructed, or very violent rapids which expose a paddler to above average endangerment. Drops may contain large, unavoidable waves and holes or steep, congested chutes with complex, demanding routes. Rapids may continue for long distances between pools, demanding a high level of fitness. What eddies exist may be small, turbulent, or difficult to reach. At the high end of the scale, several of these factors may be combined. Scouting is mandatory but often difficult. Swims are dangerous, and rescue is difficult even for experts. A very reliable eskimo roll, proper equipment, extensive experience, and practiced rescue skills are essential for survival.

CLASS VI: Extreme. One grade more difficult than Class V. These runs often exemplify the extremes of difficulty, unpredictability and danger. The consequences of errors are very severe and rescue may be impossible. For teams of experts only after close personal inspection and taking all precautions.

the same date a year earlier. In the northern Rocky Mountains, a river at the height of spring runoff may contain ten times the water it will during August. And that runoff might be twice the volume of last season's, because this past winter the snow in the high country was its deepest in 20 years. On dam-controlled rivers volume can fluctuate over the course of a day.

The Volume x Velocity Equation

The product of quantity and flow rate is expressed in cubic feet per second. CFS is not so much a vital statistic as a benchmark; it is meaningless unless applied to a specific stretch of river.

CFS tells you how a river will behave at a given reading based on how it behaved at that reading in the past — and the best way to use it is to consult with a local boater or outfitter who has experience of the behavior-CFS correlation. Like volume, CFS is not directly proportional to difficulty. A river may be unrunnable at its CFS extreme because of boat-eating rapids, and equally unrunnable at the CFS nadir because there is simply not enough water to float a boat.

The Great Falls of the Potomac River is a series of closely-spaced drops that makes for challenging Class V water.

CLASS RATINGS OF RIVERS

The class rating of a river is based on the rating of its most hellacious rapid. Bear in mind that this is a highly subjective exercise; there is no Official Board of Rapids Evaluation whose task it is to rate every formation on every river that any kayaker might attempt. A novice's "IV+" might be an expert's "III-."

To complicate matters further, class ratings take into consideration not only the rapid itself, but its situation. An isolated drop might merit a "III" — but if it is followed by 40 yards of 6-foot haystack waves, another drop into an

A quick, sure high brace combined with a draw steers this kayak clear of a possible broach.

DID YOU KNOW

To make life more interesting, volume is *not* directly proportional to any given rapid's rabidness. Rather, volume variation is nature's way of keeping you from getting bored.

You can spend a season running the same 10-mile stretch dozens of times, and never encounter exactly the same rapids, holes, eddies, and shorelines. At mid-flow, Widowmaker Falls might be a hairy drop through a narrow slot, followed by 50 yards of 4-foot standing waves. But at its peak, the rocks that made the waves may be deep-sixed, so the entire rapid is "washed out." Instead of a roller coaster, it's a waterslide that shoots your boat through at breathtaking speed but on a reassuringly calm surface.

eddy sheer bordered by a hole, and more waves before the runout, you are looking at some serious Class IV paddling.

Another aspect of rapids ratings is dependent on the term "technical." A technical rapid is usually one that is characterized by a good deal of exposed rocks. The drop may not be that great, but the course can require significant zigging and zagging.

Prior to your trip, you can make some general assumptions about a river based on its rating. For Class II, know your braces and feel secure with them; at Class III or above, be able to roll.

For your first downriver run, a Class II river with a rapid or two edging toward Class III on the scale is a reasonable compromise. It provides the hydrodynamics you'll need to practice your pool moves, and knowing that it's only second on a six-step scale is psychologically reassuring. The ideal result of a Class II maiden voyage is impatience; when you start asking, "Hey, where's the real water?," you can be confident that you are ready to progress to the intermediate stage.

WHITEWATER SAFETY

Here's Question 1 in the Whitewater Kayaker Multiple-Choice Safety Quiz:

You are eddied-out above a rapid, with cliff on one side and gentle beach on the other. In your best judgment based on your skills, experience, and mood of the moment, the rapid downstream is beyond your ability to negotiate without flipping — turbulent enough to make a successful roll iffy — and the runout is preceded by a lengthy stretch of standing waves and exposed rocks.

A: You sneak the rapid to one side, hoping that an eddy line neither grabs you nor forces you to paddle back into the channel you meant to pass up.

B: You let the most experienced member of your party run it first, and then follow her line.

C: You get it over with, hitting the vee, punching the first wave, and trusting that confidence will suddenly well up, accompanied by an adrenaline-charged vigor in your paddling.

D: You rely on destiny and your brace, figuring that even if you're not especially confident of either, you could get lucky.

There is no correct answer. The choice is up to you, but don't forget — note that gentle beach — that it includes E: None of the above. You ferry to shore, portage, and re-launch. You'll never know whether you would have made the rapid, but what the heck. Chances are you'll have another opportunity to decide whether to find out.

Walking a rapid is an example of the kayaking safety rule that's the basis for all the other safety rules: Before you need to get out of trouble, you first must get into trouble.

Safety Rule 1: When in doubt about your ability to run a rapid, walk around it.

In the same way whitewater kayaking looks more difficult to learn than it is, its danger is more perceptual than actual. The water in which you will boat is blessedly plastic: It is soft when you are going with its flow, carrying you along as if you were cradled. Yet it grows "harder" when it is cushioned against an obstacle like a rock, forming a springboard upon which you can bounce around toward freer-flowing channels.

Nonetheless, only a fool would ignore the wide latitude for mishap that remains. Most problems are avoidable through preventive medicine. We'll begin the safety lecture with them.

The reference to the safety lecture is not metaphorical. Even among an experienced party, the safety lecture helps to clear out the cobwebs left over from the complexities and diversions of workaday life, and to focus everyone's mind on the river.

The leader should review the essentials. (See Chapter 15 for some thoughts on leaders and leadership.) These include what to do if you miss an Eskimo roll and must exit the boat and swim; throw-bag techniques and responsibilities; and analysis of any problematic rapids of which party members have foreknowledge. Details on these aspects appear later in this chapter, but assisted rescue is beyond the scope of this book (for further reading on river safety and rescue, see "Sources & Resources" at the back of this book).

Another topic is making certain everyone has the signals straight. We've joked about the advantage of having another party member attempt a rapid first, but once the run is completed, that person has responsibilities in guiding the others. Different boaters have different signals — that's why it's a good idea to resolve those differences in the safety session — but there are a few ways to make signals more clear.

First, forget about hollered instructions; even a moderate rapid can be as loud as a Grateful Dead concert. Second, use your paddle as a semaphore: It's a lot longer than your arms, and it's right there. Third, signals should employ side-to-side movement, rather than back-and-forth, since the foreshort-

STOP!   STOP!   HELP! EMERGENCY!

ALL CLEAR: PROCEED DOWN THE CENTER   ALL CLEAR: PROCEED DOWN THIS WAY

UNIVERSAL RIVER SIGNALS

STOP: Potential hazard ahead. Wait for "all clear" signal before proceeding, or scout ahead. Form a horizontal bar with your outstretched arms. Those seeing the signal should pass it back to others in the party.

HELP/EMERGENCY: Assist the signaller as quickly as possible. Give three long blasts on a police whistle while waving a paddle, helmet or life vest over your head. If a whistle is not available, use the visual signal alone. A whistle is best carried on a lanyard attached to your life vest.

ALL CLEAR: Come ahead (in the absence of other directions, proceed down the center). Form a vertical bar with your paddle or one arm held high above your head. Paddle blade should be turned flat for maximum visibility. To signal direction or a preferred course through a rapid around obstruction, lower the previously vertical "all clear" by 45 degrees toward the side of the river with the preferred route. Never point toward the obstacle you wish to avoid.

ening of distance encourages misinterpretation of the latter.

Rules of the River

Now that you've got your signals down, here are some ways to cheat trouble.

RULE 1. WEAR A PFD AND A HELMET. These items are complementary, not mutually exclusive. A helmet is designed to keep you from being knocked unconscious. A Type III PFD is designed to help keep you above water. Wear both at all times.

RULE 2. OBSERVE THE DRESS CODE. If you follow the other rules, you don't need to tog up for the absolute worst-case scenario, especially if it will make you miserable. A drysuit is confining, restrictive, and hot as a toaster oven in summer weather.

Instead, base your dress on a realistic assessment of the conditions you can expect. A kayaker with plenty of Class III experience who doesn't intend to play in rapids might leave the wetsuit at home even in spring if the river is Class II; the same kayaker wears not only the wetsuit but also a paddling jacket if the river is Class IV, with canyon stretches of steep banks and long sets of big waves.

Beginners should err on the side of over-dressing, because they are going to do a lot of swimming. Don't overestimate the reliability of your Eskimo roll; when you're starting out in whitewater, you are going to learn by doing — over and over again — and that means plenty of missed rolls and time in the water. Be sensible: when you begin to become chilly —

when shivering sets in — take a rest, warm up, have a snack. Then, and only then, take another run.

RULE 3. ALCOHOL AND WATER DON'T MIX. At the end of the runout below Tumbleweed, a Class IV rapid in the Alberton Gorge of Montana's Clarkfork River, our party once rescued a waterlogged rafter from another party. He was not wearing a PFD, but he had managed to retain hold of his beer can.

Inebriation's effect on judgment accounts for a large percentage of boating accidents, but there are secondary reasons not to drink and kayak. Alcohol increases susceptibility to hypothermia and dehydration.

Get to the take-out, make camp or load your gear, and police the area for litter, yours or other persons'.

Now it's Miller time.

RULE 4. WATCH YOUR STEP. Dr. Tom Myers, a general-practice physician with the Grand Canyon Health Center and a weekend riverman, treats numerous Colorado River boaters each summer. Over half of his cases involve injuries sustained either getting to shore or once there.

Most are lower-extremity sprains or fractures, and they fall into two categories: slipping on rocks while boarding or exiting a boat, and careless side hikes in footwear suitable only for in-kayak use. Be aware of the threat, and act accordingly. And if you decide to dive off the rock for a refreshing swim, find out what's below the surface before you do; that rock you're standing on may have some underwater friends.

RULE 5. SCOUT. Many — perhaps, depending on the river, most — rapids do not require a beaching and a scramble up to a vantage point; in fact, as we learned in Rule 4, the latter presents hazards of its own. But big technical water on a new river or unfamiliar conditions on one you've boated before call for respect and reconnaissance.

If you are of average height, your eye level when you are in your kayak is about 2 feet above the water's surface. From any appreciable distance upstream, some features of a drop will be out of your line of sight. If what you can see is swirly, rocky, or steep, it's

---

YOU AND THE ELEMENTS

HYPOTHERMIA

Hypothermia is a reduction in the temperature of the body's core, and when it occurs in paddle sports, it is most likely to be a result of conduction. Conduction is the direct transfer of heat from the skin to whatever it is in contact with — and when that is cold or even cool water, conduction is unfortunately efficient; water conducts heat 240 times as well as nonmoving air of the same temperature. Even if you are not immersed, and even in air temperatures as warm as 60 degrees, stiff winds combined with constant spray and splashing can bring on hypothermia.

The visible signs of the onset of mild hypothermia include blue lips, uncontrollable shivering, fatigue, lack of coordination, and uncharacteristic irritability. Wilderness medicine expert Dr. James Wilkerson (see Sources & Resources) suggests that when hypothermia is a possibility, party members observe each other for the "umbles": The victim mumbles, fumbles, stumbles, tumbles, and grumbles.

As for treatment, Wilkerson recommends "all those things your mother told you to do when you went out in the cold." Get off the water, put on several layers of dry clothes, stomp around to restore warmth to large muscles, and drink warm beverages. If it is the only potential source of external heat, a fire might be necessary. Your companions should dig a pit for it; never fashion a stone fire-ring. Not only does it leave an unsightly mess, but water in river rocks can turn to steam and cause them to explode.

The old folk wisdom that dictates putting a victim in a sleeping bag or tarp with another person is now discouraged. In severe hypothermia, blood pools in the muscles and becomes acidic. Warmed too quickly by skin-to-skin contact, the blood can return to the heart and cause shock or cardiac arrest.

Never ignore hypothermia and

continued on page 156

allow it to advance to this stage; it is nearly impossible to treat severe hypothermia in the field. Catch it at the "umbles" stage, and you'll soon be rewarmed and ready to continue your trip.

Hypothermia's opposite, hyperthermia, is an increase in body temperature. It's less likely on the water, but if it occurs it will be of the type call "exertional,' that is, the day is very warm and humid, and you are working hard in the boat.

The first stage of hyperthermia is *heat exhaustion*, characterized by excessive sweating, damp skin, and paleness; there may also be nausea, weakness, or confusion. Body temperature goes up as high as 102 degrees. The solution is shade, rest, cold (but not iced) water mixed with a half teaspoon of salt to the quart.

Heat stroke is a medical emergency. Sweating stops, heartbeat accelerates, and lethargy and disorientation become more pronounced as body temperature passes 104

degrees. Professional treatment is indicated, but if unavailable, provide the same remedies as for heat exhaustion, and additionally wrap the victim in wet clothing. Fanning will speed heat reduction.

With *dehydration*, one symptom can be counterintuitive: You may not feel thirsty. Again, mental disorientation sets in, along with weariness. Rehydration is the cure. Because of the possible lack of thirst, an effective precaution is to monitor how often you urinate; if you haven't gone for 8 hours, you are definitely down a quart.

Dehydration can also result from diarrhea caused by lapses in hygiene. No party member should handle food, his own or food he is preparing for others, without washing his hands with soap. Use the liquid biodegradable type, do your ablutions at least 200 feet from the river. Treat the symptoms of diarrhea with over-the-counter medications and they will eventually abate, but during its course imbibe as much fluid as possible. Plain water is best.

nice to get the big picture before you forge on.

When you do, keep in mind Rule 5A: Waves and hydraulics appear smaller from above, but plenty larger when they are breaking over your bow — or head.

It isn't always necessary to leave

the boat to scout. Once you become confident that you are master of your kayaking destiny, you'll learn that you can come quite close to the head end of a formation before passing the point of no return. When you do scout a rapid from the boat, also check out the water above the rapid. Look for side eddies or

Never whitewater kayak alone. Always be keenly aware of what is happening to fellow boaters and be ready to assist them when doing so won't endanger your own life.

shallows to which you can retreat if you decide you need a different line, a portage, or a breather for deciding between the two.

RULE 6. NEVER WHITEWATER KAYAK ALONE. Boating with a companion — or several — is not only prudent, but more fun. Even better,

---

TECHNIQUE TIP

HOLDING ON

It's considered bad form to lose your paddle or your boat. It's considered worse form to lose your life.

In spring runoff a few years back, several of my rivermates and I were rowing the support raft when a friend capsized his kayak and took a swim. No more than a few yards from shore, he looked downstream at us and said, with enviable calm, "I'm letting go." He released his kayak for us to catch, and swam with his paddle to shore, where he basked in the sun to relieve the onset of symptoms of hypothermia (see page 155) that had sapped his strength so close to the bank. Meanwhile, we retrieved his boat, and neither was the worse for wear.

invite friends whose boat of choice is a larger craft, such as a raft or dory. This support boat can carry the beach blanket, beef jerky, and, in the case of an overnighter, the heavy gear, and it does double duty as your safety backup.

If one of the kayakers is the party member most familiar with the river, he goes first. Otherwise, the raft or dory is the trailblazer, and eddies-out after the runout, to signal whatever advice will help the kayaker. If the advice *doesn't* help and the kayaker swims, the support craft is there to fish him out.

When Bad Things Happen to Good Kayakers

You can look at kayaking as a competition between human and nature, and it's forgivable if you do. A river is your superior in force, volume, and willfulness, and a 10-foot-long boat with boater weighing a total of 200 pounds shouldn't have a chance against that 10-foot-high haystack wave weighing 2 tons.

But by now, with some river experience under your belt, you've seen that kayaking isn't prizefighting; a bantamweight not only can take on a heavyweight, but has the advantage in quickness, maneuverability, and pure savvy. Besides, despite the tendency to anthropomorphize a river, in reality it is just *there*, and doesn't care if you drop in or not.

That's not to say that it might not contain a few nasty surprises — but the kayaker has a few tricks of her own up her sleeve.

Self-Rescue

Ideally, self-rescue is really only a different way of saying "Eskimo roll," for, when the river capsizes you despite your best efforts at staying upright, a successful roll is by far the quickest, cleanest means of self-rescue. Practice it and perfect it; make it second nature, a move that follows capsizing as naturally as breathing in follows breathing out.

But on the river, matters don't always go the way you expect them to; even seasoned whitewater kayakers miss rolls. And wise seasoned kayakers never lose their deep respect for the power of whitewater. It is when your roll fails and you must exit the boat that two other forms of self-rescue come into play. They are: bail out and swim to shore with the boat; and bail out, ditch the boat, and swim to shore.

Eskimo Roll

It would be wishful thinking to believe that a roll after a river flip is equivalent in ease to a voluntary practice roll in a swimming pool. At the point of your flip, your paddle isn't in the setup position; the water below may be more or less turbulent; and once you do get upright, forces can conspire to re-douse you. But the basic technique of the roll doesn't change, and there are some tricks that can make it easier in combat conditions.

The ideal boat/river orientation for a roll is with bow downstream, since when you come up, you can convert your brace to a power stroke and continue on your way. If you're perpendicular instead, set up and roll on the downstream side; that's the direction in which you want your brace planted on resurfacing.

At this point, you're saying, "Wait a darned minute. I'm upside down in a rapid. How the heck am I supposed to know which way the boat is pointing?"

There are a few answers. Most involuntary flips occur with the boat in a predictable alignment with the river. One exception is coming down face-first from an ender, but by the time you become advanced enough to do enders in the first place, you'll begin to see patterns in your landings.

Otherwise, one of three conditions is the cause of most flips:

First, you are surfing a wave, slapping braces left and right for balance — and you miss a brace. In this case, you are facing upstream. The roll is no more challenging in this position; you need only bear in mind as you execute it that you might come up in the current, and facing backwards. If you have boat-scouted and know there are no rocks or holes, you can take the rapid in this position. Otherwise, do a 180-degree turn with a crisp high-brace pivot on the downstream side, and continue on your way.

Second, you are shooting standing waves and fail to power over the top of a big whitecap. It's likely that when the wave pushes you back and over it will also throw you off trim; in addition, the trough will collaborate in turning you sideways to the river. Set up and roll for a downstream brace.

Third, you are in trim but a side wave or eddy line proves to be the superior of your brace. Here you are likely to remain in trim (that is, bow facing downstream) after you dump. A roll will take advantage of this situation.

Another part of the answer to the question of how you can figure your position after a flip is to predict it in advance. You won't want to become overconfident ('Even if that one flips me, I can see how I'll end up, and my roll will be a piece of cake'), nor do you want to be defeatist ('That one is sure to flip me, and in that mess of a rapid, I'll probably have to swim'). Rather, realistically evaluate the chances that a particular hydraulic will do a particular thing and, if it does, where you will find yourself as a result.

The Hesitation Roll

Once you feel confident enough to know that you will jack yourself back up, add the hesitation roll to your repertory. If the water that flipped you is particularly roily, its aeration might provide insufficient support for your brace. Set up at your leisure — and then wait a few seconds for the river to move you to firmer downstream water before you sweep. While you are standing by, you will probably be turned sideways to the river. You'll have time to feel the direction of the current, decide on which flank to roll (downstream), and have an idea of what to expect after you do.

Safe Swimming

If you miss your roll and come out of the boat, you've got a few chores to

Correct Swimming Posture. Swimming technique for the whitewater kayaker is meant to prevent injury should he hit a rock. His feet are headed downstream so that he can push off of obstacles with them and prevent injury to other more vulnerable parts of the body. His head is up so that he can scout for holes, rocks, or sweepers and attempt to avoid them by using his arms and hands as rudders.

attend to, most notably swimming safely in whitewater. On a river, you don't have to turn your attention to emptying your boat and reboarding, as you must in open water. But there is plenty to think about.

The human/capsized kayak combination is notably unsleek, so you will move more slowly than the river itself. And shore, where you'll eventually land, is rarely distant in a whitewater river, although it can be inhospitable; cliffs can make for tough landings, and coming ashore amidst sweepers is courting disaster. But before you concern yourself with the shoreline, you need to know how to safely swim a rapid.

It's best to hold on to your boat and paddle, but it should go without saying that abandoning your equipment is preferable to holding on to it if doing so could endanger your life.

Assuming swimming for shore with your gear is not problematic, as you resurface, grab the coaming of your boat and swing it around in front of you perpendicular to the flow and downstream from you. Never swim

with the boat upstream from you; it could pin you against a rock or strainer. Finally, as you approach shore, if the water is moving with any force, don't try to stand up until it is no more than knee-deep.

BROACHING

And then there was the time that Bob Carson tried to drown his mother. . .

Carson and Mom were negotiating, in an open canoe, a technical section of the Big Blackfoot. This stretch is a good 200 yards of "rock garden," a significant drop studded with exposed boulders requiring a good deal of zigging and zagging. Carson zigged when he should have zagged, and his canoe became broadside to a sharp granite spire.

The late summer day and the water were warm, and Carson and Mom were both experienced boaters. They hit the drink and made it to shore without difficulty. A minute later, the canoe buckled around the rock like aluminum foil on a baked potato. The upside is that Carson's boatmate now gets to introduce him to strangers as "my son the lawyer, who once tried to drown me."

Within the confines of a kayak instead of an open canoe, the danger of a broach is more pronounced. The loudest wake-up call on the power of moving water comes the first time you see (or, worse, are in) a boat pinned sideways against a rock. Assuming the kayak is fashioned of fiberglass, and friendly anglers or other boaters are downstream, you'll be reunited with your craft — but expect the bow half to come to a stop at Traveler's Rest Eddy, while the stern half continues on all the way to Big Bend Shoals.

The force of water holding a boat against an obstacle is equal to the area presented multiplied by water velocity times the constant 2.8. For a 14-foot kayak held hull-upstream, presenting one 25-square-foot side to water traveling at 5 miles per hour, this works out to about:

$$25 \times 5 \times 2.8 = 350 \text{ pounds of pressure}$$

If you aren't a world-class weightlifter, this is a formula for disaster. Because most water/rock formations result in a pillow that wants to push a boat away, broaching is unlikely; at the same time, it is, along with a hole and a sweeper, one of the three most lethal perils on the river.

A subset of being pinned against a single rock is the broach in which stern and bow are stuck against two separate rocks with current between them. The result is "window-shading,"

Broaching. Note how this kayaker is leaning downstream. If he tilts upstream, he may be flipped by the current, and possibly pinned in a much more dangerous upside-down position. Using his paddle (and even his hand, a good reason to wear neoprene gloves), he can fend off the rock and proceed downstream.

a term colorful in its description and unpleasant in its occurrence. You are in for a swim.

When a side-pin against a rock becomes inevitable, immediately tilt downstream toward the rock. Brace yourself with your hand against its face and lift your upstream hip high enough to turn the edge on that side above the rush of the oncoming water. If you don't, the current will push down on your upstream side, flipping you in that direction. There is a good chance of being caught halfway over, so you are presenting even more hull area to the broaching rock.

At the slightest indication that the boat is deforming — if you even *think* it is — abandon ship *without hesitation*. To do so, first free your skirt with your non-bracing hand, then flip upstream and boost yourself free of the boat as you do so. The move must be quick and clean; you want to be mostly out of the kayak before the flip is complete.

If the current is relatively mild

and there are no signs of boat deformation, you can try to free yourself. Using the brace hand — and keeping the bottom of the boat facing upstream — push forward and backwards, the same way you'd rock a vehicle stuck in snow. As you do, it's a good idea to scout the rest of the rapid; if your stern frees first, you might have to ride the waves backwards.

HOLES

No river feature is more violently chaotic than a hole. The feeling as you are pulled from your boat and descend into one is that the water is clawing at you, that it wants to eat your helmet and tear off your PFD, and then proceed to strip you bare, after which it can chew on your corpus at its leisure. If you are able to look up, you'll see the blue of the sky turn to pitch-black as you bottom-out.

Fortunately, this is the point at which you will make a graceful departure. Holes form at the bottoms of ledges and dams, but on the typical river you are more likely to encounter one behind a good-sized rock. A hole is an infill: Water coming from upstream is pushed to either side of the boulder and wants to continue downstream. Gravity, however, dictates that some of it must dump into the vacuum behind the rock.

If the drop is significant, this dump is abrupt and forceful, with the infilling water plunging down along the face of the rock. But what goes down *will* come up; at the base of the hole

the power tuckers out, and the water now flows away from the rock, downstream and out of the turbulence.

Here is where you will find the "This Way Out" sign. The key to reaching this exit is to relax, and you are more likely to do so if you visualize going into a hole before it happens, because it is undeniably frightening.

As you are sucked down, determine which way is up, while fighting the urge to try to go in that direction. The water will grow darker as you descend. You may also be able to reach out and feel the face of the rock as you pass it.

At the bottom of the hole, you will be moved away from the rock. To ensure your release at this point, dive even lower with a strong breaststroke. Finally, as you feel the downstream flow becoming constant, swim for the surface, toward which your PFD will be taking you anyway.

Holes are a river's ogres, and, like all hazards, are best handled through avoidance. Local inquiry is always a prudent idea. Holes do exist on otherwise boatable rivers that are powerful enough to make inextricable entrapment a real possibility. By definition, this is expert water and should not be attempted by intermediates unless a wide berth is available for skirting the hole.

VARIATIONS ON A THEME

F rom the days long before the Russians first looked upon the boat they called the *baidarka*, both the design of kayaks and their uses have constantly evolved, and probably always will. While some of today's variations are for experts, there's no reason why you might not someday be one. That guy shooting off a waterfall was, just like you, once struggling to master his first Eskimo roll.

NEW HORIZONS

The uses and configurations of kayaks are limited only by kayakers' imaginations — and kayakers tend to be imaginative sorts. Here are a few takes on both design and kayaking activities, presented roughly in order of expertise required.

Kayaking à Deux

The tandem kayak (or K-2) is, excepting the types used in competition, a touring boat with two cockpits set in line. Besides being a craft of togetherness — when you are oohing and aahing at the scenery, it's nice to have someone to ooh and aah with — the weight of two people increases stability and the tandem kayak provides more cargo room. The extra weight, by the way, is more than offset by the combined two-person paddle power.

A rudder is close to mandatory in a tandem, and is usually controlled by the rear paddler's foot pedals. Like the K-1, some tandems can be sail-mounted, or catted into a four-person boat; the latter is about as stable as a barge. If there is a disadvantage to the tandem, it's in increased difficulty in transporting and

paddled without a partner if you choose. All have excellent initial stability.

Most of all, inflatables are fun and highly accessible. Many professional rafting guides carry inflatables, because they can confidently put a relatively green client into one with minimal shore instruction. Slalom kayakers may hold a slight disdain for inflatables, but you're missing a good time if you pass up the opportunity to give one a try.

This cata-kayak is a bizarre hybrid of a "traditional" cata-kayak (if there is such a thing) and an open-cockpit model. These boats are nearly impossible to capsize and are unsinkable.

Although the inflatable is usually considered a river "play" boat,

portaging, although models that break down into two or three parts go a ways toward ameliorating the problem.

Inflatables

Inflatable kayaks are tube-constructed boats that come in a surprising variety of designs. Some are rockered to as much as a 1½-foot rise at bow and stern, and are thereby nearly as maneuverable as rigid boats. Others are essentially flat-bottomed, and more suitable to Class II water. Inflatables are marketed in one- and two-person considerations, and the latter can be

there are a few models with enclosing decks that, with some ingenuity, can be packed with enough gear for extended touring. Randel Washburne, in *The Coastal Kayaker's Manual* (see Sources & Resources), includes a photo of one of the latter, belonging to Audrey Sutherland. A veteran sea kayaker, she has paddled thousands of miles of coastal water in her inflatable.

Whitewater Touring

It's possible to load enough gear into a whitewater kayak to support an overnight trip, or even a trip spanning

The downriver kayak is a specialized craft. It is a high-volume, flat-keeled boat designed to run directly downstream against the clock in an aquatic version of downhill skiing. Here is a tandem model.

several nights, as long as you are a minimalist. A number of manufacturers offer cargo bags that also serve as flotation, cunningly designed to fit into all available space you are not yourself occupying.

However, it is rarely worth the hassle. Since slalom kayaks don't feature bulks and hatch covers, all gear must be inserted — and extracted — via the cockpit. You'll want to make sure — before your trip — that you can get the bags in and get them out; for the rear, you'll have to either free the backstrap or work awkwardly around it.

A second disadvantage is that gear weight has a tendency to put the boat out of trim. Imbalance toward the stern impedes your wave-surfing ability, enders become out of the question, forward momentum is compromised, and your exposure to being grabbed by a hole is enhanced.

Whitewater touring is more hassle-free if you team up with a larger support boat. Let the canoe, raft, or Mackenzie-type dory slog downstream with the heavy stuff, while you stop to dance in the play waves.

Downriver Kayaks

The downriver kayak is predominantly a racing boat. It's shaped like an elongated diamond, with the flare behind the cockpit. Downriver kayaks have highly tippy initial stability but excellent directional stability — and they do fly.

Ocean Surfing

Early surf-riding ocean kayakers used traditional closed boats and some still do, but there are obvious dangers associated with being driven toward ocean bottom in a cocoon. More preferable for this pursuit are open (non-decked) boats, which are essentially platforms constructed of foam covered with a plastic sheath.

In this model, the surfer sits atop the boat, with the only confinement a pair of footstraps. In warm water (or in cold water with the proper dress), this kayak is a diverting addition to the surfer's quiver.

Competitive Sport

Kayakers play three general categories of games in competition, all within the skills of an intermediate boater.

The down-river race for slalom-style boats (in contrast to the dedicated downriver kayak, discussed above) is one of the few kayak pursuits in which strength and conditioning *do* count. Paddling 10 miles in an hour makes definite demands on your upper-body power and cardiovascular system. But technique plays a significant role, too: Choosing the optimal strokes, executing them with the least effort, and reading the river's fastest line all contribute to getting you to the finish first.

A slalom-gate event takes place over a short course, perhaps 50 yards of river that will include a variety of whitewater challenges. The targets through which you are aiming to shoot consist of two poles hanging from lines running from shore to shore (high enough not to clothesline anyone, please, if you happen to be constructing a course). They must be run

The kayaker's answer to slalom skiing. The slalom-gate event takes place over a short course, about 50 yards of river carefully selected to test the racer's abilities.

in a prescribed order, and success requires some upstream paddling and a lot of high-brace and Duffek work. Standings are determined by time, with penalty seconds added for missing gates or brushing their poles.

The third event, rodeo, is arguably the most fun for kayaker and spectator alike. This is a freestyle "show-off" contest. The ideal venue is a defined hydrodynamic feature with a strong back-eddy current flowing up toward it along one shore; a non-undercut ledge, for example, almost always provides both. Some compulsory moves may be involved, but innovation and ingenuity are always part of the game. Contestants surf forward, backward, and sideways; pop enders; and exploit the water to the extent of their ability and imagination. At the conclusion of each go-around (usually each boater gets several turns), the kayaker peels out and heads downstream, catches the eddy, and queues up for the next try; after the last turn, the really cool kayaker tosses away her paddle, capsizes on purpose, and comes up with a hands-only roll.

Local kayak retailers are excellent sources of information about competitive events in your area.

Squirt Boats

True squirt boats have been around for about a dozen years, and they take the sport into — way into — the expert's territory. This kayak (and though it is a kayak, its only proper name is "squirt boat") is roughly similar in shape to a slalom model, but in the sense of "wearing" your boat, the squirt is a skintight suit. Length is significantly reduced, and volume can be less than half of a slalom boat's, as little as 24 gallons.

In the squirt-boat trade-off, stability is sacrificed without compromise to the gods of maneuverability.

The squirt boat's name comes from the ease with which it can perform its basic move: In hydraulics a larger boat would barely feel, a squirt boater can often rear back or plunge forward to bury stern or bow cockpit-deep — and then "squirt." Squirters take advantage of subsurface currents inaccessible to other boats; in some hydraulics it's possible to "float" the entire boat underwater.

Clearly, a kayak so small that it can do tricks in small water is able to do major-league magic in big water — whether in control of the kayaker or not. A vivid vocabulary has evolved for squirt moves and mishaps, including "boof," "cartwheel," "green-lean," "meltdown," "Schnitz," "Swirl-O-Gram," and the ever-popular "black attack," cryptically defined by squirt expert James E. Snyder (see Sources & Resources) as "a controlled, spinning, vertical exit to a total submersion mystery move."

First Descents

The concept of first descents of rivers derived from the climber's first ascents of mountains; in fact, Yvon Chouinard, the skilled mountaineer and innovative equipment designer, turned from the slopes to the whitewater in his middle years and continued to score firsts. The idea, to paraphrase a pop-culture cliché, is to boat boldly where no person has boated before.

Boldly is the key word here; the reason any peak or river is unconquered is that it is potentially unconquerable. In the case of whitewater, first-descent candidates are at best Class VI+, at worst off the scale. And as the American Whitewater Affiliation defines Class VI water (see pages 146-148), it is "nearly impossible and very dangerous. . .[and] for teams of experts only, after close study and with all precautions taken."

The "squirt" boat is for experts only. It is the quintessential playboat, designed to allow daredevil kayakers to laugh in the face of truly wild hydraulics.

While you likely will not attempt any first descents, the last phrase of the AWA definition provides an occasion for reminder: Close study and precautions, as I've emphasized throughout this book, are never poor ideas. For the everyday kayaker, every new river is a first descent, and if you are moving up from Class III to Class IV, take a tip from the first-descenders: Know all you can about the water, and remember that the top end of precaution is to walk around, rather than run, any given hell-roarer.

Pushing the Envelope

Running waterfalls appears to be, as you watch intrepid plungers on some TV special, a point-and-shoot proposition: You place your bet and you take your chances. It actually involves a wealth of both scouting and technique and, when precautions are taken, is more daring than dangerous. Falls dozens of feet high have even been run in open canoes, albeit filled to the gunwales with air bags and piloted by pros who can roll these (to the kayaker) unwieldy beasts.

Most likely your experience will be with waterfalls measured in the dozens of inches, but again, you can benefit from what the experts have learned. Assess a drop by the distance from its horizon line to the point where the water reappears; if it's appreciable, you must know in advance what you can't see at the moment. Scouting is compulsory, and it puts you in an excellent position, situationally and psychologically. If there is a clean route that you judge within your skills, you can accept the challenge, but if not, you're already out of the boat and ready to portage.

T H E
E Q U A T I O N S
O F   K A Y A K I N G

athematicians have failed us. There should be a branch of calculation that solves outdoor-adventuring formulas, such as:

$$K \times C \times P_g \times D = L$$

where, on a backpacking trip,

K = number of kids,

C = kids' capacity for crankiness,

P_g = patience of grown-ups in the face of C, and

D = dogs in the party

equate to

L = lateness of arrival at campsite

Our calculus of kayaking begins with three axiomatic formulas. It's a whimsical way to approach three factors — one mechanical and two very human — that go to the heart of both whitewater and touring.

Shuttling Science

$$K/(B_r \times V) + (P/C_p) = S$$

where, to get from take-out to put-in at the end of a trip,

K = number of kayaks,

B_r = boat-rack capacity,

V = number of vehicles with racks,

P = number of people, and

C_p = passenger capacity of cars without racks

equate to

S = successful shuttle

Shuttling is the process of doubling back, usually by vehicle, for purposes of off-water transport of the party. In other words, when your kayaking trip ends, there must be at least one rig waiting for you. This is not a concern on open-water trips in

Shuttling science. It entails arriving at your put-in location with all the boats and gear and having adequate transportation waiting for you at your take-out location downstream.

which the put-in and the take-out are the same, but running downriver or touring overnight, you are invariably launching at one point and landing at another.

Eavesdropping on a kayaking party's discussion of which vehicles end up where is not unlike listening to Abbott and Costello's "Who's on First?" routine. Typically you'll hear couplets like: "We can leave Fred's car at the take-out," followed by "Yeah, but what do we do with the boats?" But it doesn't have to be quite that goofy, if approached logically.

For illustration, consider a whitewater day trip; longer shuttles, or those for touring, use the same principles.

Let's assume six kayakers; two Chevy pickup trucks and a Jeep Cherokee, each with a rack that can accommodate two kayaks; and a mid-seventies model Ford sedan that, despite a few springs poking out of rips in the upholstery, can seat four people.

On a river trip, roads usually run along the same valley as the watercourse. Relative to your departure point, you may drive upstream or downstream to reach your put-in point, and the shuttle is slightly different in the two cases. If you get to the put-in first, you do the actual shuttling before launching; if the road runs upstream, it's done afterward.

ARRIVING FROM UPSTREAM. Gear is

ALTERNATIVE SHUTTLING

Especially on a day trip when your party is small and your gear minimal, it's possible to make the put-in/take-out traverse without dropping a take-out vehicle.

If the overland route between the two points is open highway, hitchhiking might be a modality with which you are uncomfortable. But backcountry range roads or gravel tracks are not a great risk, and on many that parallel popular rivers, the traffic is mostly fellow boaters doing their own shuttle. Wear your PFD to signal why you are standing there with your thumb out, and few people will pass you by if they have room for one more. And remember that if you are the driver in this situation, you are obligated to give that hitchhiker a lift.

The truly hardy kayaker — you know the sort, someone who can't get enough exercise — might want to jog from take-out back to put-in. A less exerting alternative, especially if you are approaching from downstream, is to lock a mountain bike to a tree at the take-out. Pedal upstream, rack the two-wheeler or toss it in the back of your truck, and you're on your way.

For multiple-day trips, consider a shuttle service. On the Main Fork of Idaho's Salmon River, for example, you can expect to spend 5 days waterbound — and 2 days, plus motel tariffs, getting your vehicles from one end to the other, since highway configuration mandates the round-trip at about 400 miles even though the river-run is only 75 miles.

In similar cases, you might have two alternatives. On the Salmon, jet boats are available to rendezvous with you at a set time to transport you and your gear back upstream. The service tends to be expensive, however, and you may feel that using it is environmentally insensitive. Most commercial powerboat pilots are courteous, careful to watch for non-motorized craft, and cut their speed and wake when they pass. Still, their unavoidable noise and engine exhaust are perhaps antithetical to the wilderness experience.

Instead, consider patronizing an agency that provides drivers to handle the shuttle for you. They are highly reliable. You'll find your vehicles parked at your landing with keys stashed in the pre-arranged hiding place, and you'll be providing employment for a proverbially impoverished college lad or lass.

unloaded at the put-in and then all four vehicles proceed to the take-out. The three racked rigs remain there, while the shuttle drivers return in the Ford. When the river trip is complete, the Ford driver is dropped off to retrieve his vehicle on the way home.

By now you are getting the idea that shuttling is a lot like the old riddle of the fox, chicken, and sack of grain that must be transported across a river in a boat that will hold only two of the three — and if either the fox and the chicken or the chicken and the grain are left alone, one will eat the other. But then, it was never a very difficult riddle.

ARRIVING FROM DOWNSTREAM. In this case, the take-out is reached first, where the Ford is dropped, its driver boards one of the Chevys, and all party members proceed to the put-in. At the end of the trip, four people head back to the put-in in the Ford to shuttle the racked rigs.

That's pretty much all there is to it, aside from two cautions. First, either at put-in or take-out, any party members not shuttling are assigned to see to the gear, theirs and the others'. For example, at the put-in boats should be carried down to riverside, airbags inflated, PFDs and spray skirts dealt out to the kayaks to which they belong, and as many chores as possible accomplished to help make the trip go smoothly.

Second, door and ignition keys should be hidden on the take-out vehicle, and during the pre-launch safety lecture all party members *must*

be informed of the keys' location. If one of your kayakers is injured or otherwise needs help, your two strongest boaters must head for assistance with all dispatch. Should they reach the car and be unable to use it for want of a key, a mishap can turn into a disaster.

The Tsimis-to-Fun Ratio

$$T/F = S_q$$

where a given expedition involves some effort,

T = tsimis in putting a trip together and

F = on-river fun

equate to

S_q = satisfaction quotient

The solution of this equation will never be zero, and you must learn to live with that fact. *Tsimis*, a handy Yiddish term that is most connotatively translated as "hassle," is a part of any outdoors experience, and that's not necessarily a negative.

Mike Sherwood, an expert runner of western Montana rivers, provides an astute observation on the attraction of backcountry pursuits in general. "First, you get to go somewhere," Sherwood says. "Second, you get to do and see stuff, and third, you get to go home."

Sherwood's point is that hassle is not some obstacle to be overcome, but rather is integral to the experience. The satisfaction, efficiency, and success of a well-organized trip increase your appreciation for all of its aspects — and for the comforts of returning to your cozy abode.

The overriding factor in bringing

the *T/F* ratio down to its irreducible minimum is sensitivity — to yourself, and to your mates.

A place to begin is to have your stuff together. Know what you will need on the water, and where to find it pre-trip. Here is where the much-scorned list shines.

Whitewater Gear

This list covers the typical trip in which actual on-river time from put-in to take-out is 3 or 4 hours.

FOR BOAT AND BOATER
Kayak
Paddle
Flotation bags
Spray skirt
Personal flotation device
Helmet

CLOTHING
Drysuit
Wetsuit
Polypropylene jersey
Paddling jacket
Booties, sandals, or high-top sport shoes
Gloves
Nose clips
Sunglasses
Eyeglass safety strap
Daypack containing dry clothing (leave in vehicle that is parked at the take-out)

PERSONAL GEAR
1-quart water bottle
In a ditty bag or dry bag, capacity about $^1/_2$ cubic foot:
First aid kit
Swiss Army-type knife
Toilet tissue

Disposable cigarette lighter
Pen and pad
High-energy snack
Sun-protection lotion
Insect repellant
Lip balm
Water-purification tablets
$2 in small change

Touring Gear

Taking advantage of the greater cargo capacity, let's have this trip cover the better part of a full day. To the whitewater list, add the following.

FOR BOAT AND BOATER
Pump
Sponge
Painter line
Dry bags
Sea anchor
Repair kit

FOR SAFETY AND NAVIGATION
Compass
Maps and map case
Tide and current tables
Whistle or horn
Flashlight or flares
Portable shelter (for example, space blanket)
Throw-bag

PERSONAL GEAR
Lunch
Biodegradable hand soap
Hat
Binoculars
Camera and extra film
Fishing equipment

SUPPORT RAFT

With your cargo space significantly

increased, you can upgrade from standard class to a luxury cruise.

To the preceding two lists, add these:

Second throw-bag

Bailer (make one by cutting the bottom off a 1-gallon plastic jug)

Cooler with regular or "blue" ice

A sumptuous luncheon repast

Disposable plates, glasses, and utensils

Large plastic bag for trash

Icepick

Finally, reduce *tsimis* by being sensitive to other party members. This is no more than minding the advice of your kindergarten teacher: It's nice to work and play well with others. You'll find more detail in the discussion of leadership below, but a few considerations should be kept in mind, all of which involve punctiliousness. Show up on time at the trip's meeting place; have your gear in order and your vehicle fueled; pitch in on whatever must be done; and, above all, be cheerful in the face of adversity.

The Leadership Logarithm

$$E + S + J + \sqrt{C} = L$$

where a leader is to be chosen for a given expedition,

E = experience,

S = sensitivity,

J = judgment, and

C = consensus

equate to

L = leadership

Kent Madin of Baja Expeditions in San Diego, an adventure-travel firm that includes in its offerings tour-kayaking in the Sea of Cortez, ponders the question of what to look for in a leader: "A swagger stick and a well-clipped mustache," Madin decides.

He's kidding. "The leader," he continues, "is the person who can articulate the purpose and the plan. Leadership is having a handle on all aspects of the trip."

Judgmental decisions don't necessarily begin and end on the river. "Conflict can be the make-it or break-it of a friendship," Madin adds. "But if it's a question of danger, I'd rather be alive with one fewer friend."

Conflict is hardly inevitable, although over the course of many kayaking trips it can arise. But it's best resolved by avoiding it in the first place, through consensual discussion, realistic evaluation of the situation and your skills and those of your mates, and responsiveness to everyone's needs and concerns.

A self-aware initiate into the boating fraternity knows that every member of a party is a leader in given circumstances, of herself and of others. At the put-in of a mixed-craft trip including several novices, you'll note them falling into several types. One might "stay out of the way"; another will ask what he can do; a third observes the what and how of tasks to be accomplished, and pitches in without asking. Endeavor to fall into the last of these categories.

As the seasoned hand, you can go about your chores while resenting the slackers, or you can take a moment to lead by suggesting ways they can help.

Choose the latter and you'll not only be greasing the trip's wheels, but educating the neophyte.

Most situations involving leadership are similar, in that they will far more often respond to mechanics, interpersonal relationships, or minor irritations,

The leadership logarithm: There is not necessarily one leader in a party of white-water kayakers, but it is important to safe, enjoyable outings that each member's strengths and weaknesses be sorted out *before* the kayaks enter the water.

rather than true danger. When the wind comes up and the temperature drops 20 degrees, for example, each boater should lead by example.

Everyone is less comfortable, but whining won't make the sun come out. The more cheerful you remain, and the more sympathetic support you provide to a less-experienced partner, the

TECHNIQUE TIP

LEAVE THE GLASS AT HOME

Two tips: First, do not carry glass containers. Food that comes in bottles — the pickles to garnish your sandwiches, for example — should be repackaged in plastic containers, and pack only canned beverages. Should you break a glass bottle, your most careful policing of the area will still leave shards. That's an insult both to the environment and to the next party of boaters that arrives at this beach.

Second, here's a neat cooler trick. Instead of using blue ice or ice cubes, fill a couple of clean half-gallon plastic milk jugs with water to 80 percent of capacity and freeze overnight. When you stop for lunch, cut the top from one and decant meltage into your water bottle. Now the mysterious icepick comes into play. Hack at the ice and —

Viola! The beverages are served. Would you like one cube or two, madam?

⁇

harder it becomes for him to complain. In the face of any inexorable and unpleasant condition, you have two options when a companion turns sullen: You can bully him into submission, or you can elicit good behavior by your own behavior and verbal support. Guess which method is usually more effective?

Even on a professionally guided trip, in which your outfitters are the putative leaders (and indeed, in acute situations, their word rules), self-leadership is an obligation you have to your guide and your fellow clients. Listen to the former, and act collegially toward the latter. Having paid for the expedition you expect expertise, and the vast majority of established pros will provide it in spades. But if you are demanding and purely lazy, you're displaying an arrogance that is inappropriate for the wilderness experience.

Leadership, in the best of all possible kayaking worlds, takes the form of support and advice. Sure, you might run into a friend whose idea of tutoring is to scream, as a standing wave hangs you up and threatens to topple you, "Paddle, you chowderhead!" More often, while eddied-out upstream you'll get some gentle advice, such as "That first haystack is pushy. When you hit it, make sure you've got some steam up — and don't forget to paddle, you chowderhead!" An offer to run a rapid first to show a beginner the line, to eddy-out and stand by for support, or simply to reassure that what looks like a boat-eater isn't really that bad — all are easily made and gratefully accepted gestures of leadership.

Effective leaders keep an eye not only on the water but on the party as a whole and its individual members. A novice preoccupied with hydraulic challenge may miss signs of hypothermia, dehydration, or weariness; her mentor must not.

A good leader is a skilled psychologist. Despite its relative safety, no one turns to kayaking unless her soul is that of an adventurer. When a novice's attitude goes beyond gung-ho to foolhardy, it's the leader's role to rein her in.

formerly a ranger at Glacier National Park, codifies this principle with regard to hiking, but it applies to kayaking as well. "Plan an itinerary that you can handle," he advises, "then once you're out there don't hesi-

Leadership plus teamwork equals camaraderie and good fun both on the stream and on the way to the stream.

This is ticklish business. On the one hand, you don't want to discourage intrepidness; on the other hand, you are responsible for not encouraging rashness. Your judgment call must be based on a realistic assessment of the solution to another equation, one which balances the chance for mishap against the other boater's skills, experience, and attitude.

The leader should remind his charges that no one must attempt any challenge if they'd prefer not to — and bear in mind that that applies to the leader as well. Judgment is inherently a function of flexibility. Jim Bellamy,

tate to change the plan."

"The more narrow your definition of success, the more likely you are to fail," says Kent Madin. It's an elegant way of restating that you've never "gotta" do that Class IV whirler because of peer or self-pressure. "A little humility in all of our endeavors," Madin adds, goes a long way toward keeping followers safe, and leaders secure in their decisions.

Finally, the notion of being blessed with luck is a false friend and a worthless predictor of a leader or of a student's odds. Flipping a penny nine times and tossing "heads" has no effect on the probability of a tenth toss coming up heads — nor does making nine Class IV rapids without hitting a rock affect your chances of collision on the tenth. "People good at being lucky can end up cocky," Madin says, and that is exactly the moment when luck has an irksome tendency to run out.

As you build your confidence and notch more trips on your paddle, you'll come to notice that in private, non-guided trips, leadership is mutable and evanescent. One wonders if Karl Marx was thinking of kayaking when he wrote that contributions to the success of an enterprise should be "from each according to his abilities, to each according to his needs."

With reasonable attention to the mandates of self-leadership, the formal appointment of a commodore of the fleet is rarely necessary. Instead, you're served by exploiting abilities and attending to needs.

The kayaker who has run the river the most times may lead through the biggest rapids, but so might the person with the most all-around confidence and expertise. If an accident happens — a broached boat, say, or a kayaker perched on a mid-river rock — the recovery leader could be the person who has performed this rescue before, or the one with the coolest head, or the best throwing arm, or a troika of all three.

It's the same in less acute circumstances. Without tedious consultation, the former Eagle Scout with a merit badge in knots is the ramrod for tasks requiring ropes, from roof-rack tie-downs to on-river jerry-rigging. The graduate of a Red Cross course takes charge in case of injury or illness. The weight-lifter muscles back upstream to check on laggard party members.

And the best cook makes the stew — plus, according to long-accepted river rules, gets to watch the sunset in quiet contemplation interrupted only by the occasional imperious order to the post-dinner cleanup crew.

EPILOGUE

Kayakers tend to bore non-kayakers.

Consider: You turn the last page of a wonderfully compelling novel, and holler for your spouse. "You absolutely must read this," you say.

The credits roll at the end of a movie so transporting that your mouth remains agape and your chin on your chest long after the house lights come up. For the next week, your friends consistently flee from your insistence that they see this film right now.

As you summit Exhaustion Peak, the world is spread out below you. After taking in the view, your next move is to descend, hit the phone, and tell all your pals that if they haven't seen the vista from Exhaustion, they haven't lived.

Once you reach the "gotta" point — gotta try this, gotta experience the thrill of your first roll, gotta get out on that river or shore break — you can be assured of two things:

First, you are inducted into the ranks of the bore.

Second, you are inducted into the ranks of a pursuit that, in its permutations, will provide variety and enjoyment for the rest of your days.

Enjoy — and go ahead and press your case. Today's bore is tomorrow's prophet of kayaking.

SOURCES & RESOURCES

After reading this book you may be ready to start a new hobby, perhaps even a new obsession. If, however, you need to read more, join a club, or browse a magazine, we've set out enough information with addresses and phone numbers below to whet your appetite. We start with the major national paddling organizations and groups concerned with related topics.

ORGANIZATIONS

These leading organizations provide a wealth of information for the novice kayaker.

AMERICAN CANOE ASSOCIATION (ACA)

7432 Alban Station Rd.
Ste. B-226
Springfield, VA 22150
703-451-0141
National governing body for canoe and kayak activity. 13 regional and 250 local affiliated groups. Sponsors races and classes and provides extensive information as well as publications.

AMERICAN WHITEWATER AFFILIATION (AWA)

PO Box 85
Phoenicia, NY 12464
914-688-5569
Promotes whitewater safety, technique, equipment, and river access programs. Also publishes *American Whitewater*.

NATIONAL ORGANIZATION FOR RIVER SPORTS (NORS)

212 W. Cheyenne Mountain Blvd.
Colorado Springs, CO 80906
719-579-8754
Promotes all whitewater sports, conservation and lobbying before government agencies. Membership includes the quarterly journal, *Currents*.

UNITED STATES CANOE ASSOCIATION (USCA)

c/o Jim Mack
606 Ross St.
Middletown, OH 45044
513-422-3739
For individuals interested in canoeing and kayaking. The USCA's Five-Star Program — Competition-Cruising-Conservation-Camping-Camaraderie — highlights their concerns.

AMERICA OUTDOORS (AO)

(formerly Eastern Prof. Outfitters Assoc. and Western River Guides Association)
PO Box 1348
Knoxville, TN 37901
615-524-4814
For professional recreation service outfitters. Good source for outfitters and buying information.

AMERICAN RIVERS

(formerly American Rivers Conservation Council)
801 Pennsylvania Ave, SE
Suite 400
Washington, D.C. 20003
202-547-6900
A public interest organization working for river protection. Several publications.

EASTERN PROFESSIONAL FRIENDS OF THE RIVER (FOR)

909 12th St., No. 207
Sacramento, CA 95814
916-442-3155
Individuals and environmental groups united to preserve the great waters. Wide-ranging activities.

NATIONAL ASSOCIATION OF CANOE LIVERIES AND OUTFITTERS (NACLO)
US 27 & Hornbeck Rd.
Box 248
Butler, KY 41006
606-472-2205
Renters and outfitters.

SCHOOLS
Here are a few of the leading schools. For a more complete listing see Richard Penny's *The Whitewater Sourcebook* or the back pages of paddling magazines.

BILL DVORAK'S KAYAK AND RAFTING EXPEDITIONS
17921 US Highway 285
Nathrop, CO 81236
719-539-6851

BOULDER OUTDOOR CENTER
2510 N. 47th St.
Boulder, CO 80301
800-364-9376

NANTAHALA OUTDOOR CENTER
US 19 West, Box 41
Bryson City, NC 28713
704-488-2175

L.L. BEAN
Outdoor Discovery Program
Freeport, ME 04033
1-800-341-4341, ext.6666

OTTER BAR KAYAK SCHOOL
Box 120
Forks of Salmon, CA 96031
916-462-4772

RIVERSPORT SCHOOL OF PADDLING
213 Yough St.
Confluence, PA 15424
814-395-5744

SUNDANCE KAYAK SCHOOL AND EXPEDITIONS
14894 Galice Road
Merlin, OR 97532
503-479-8508

WILD WATERS
PO Box 157
Route 28 at the Glen
Warrensburg, NY 12885
518-494-3393

TOUR ORGANIZERS & GUIDES
There are dozens of kayak tour organizers — for both whitewater and touring venues — in North America. We recommend that you get a list from the trade organization America Outdoors (see page 181 for address). Meanwhile, here is a short list of top tour organizers we can recommend.

ALASKA DISCOVERY
369 South Franklin
Juneau, AK 99801
907-586-1911
Fax: 907-586-2332
Glacier Bay National Park, Icy Bay, Hubbard Glacier

BAJA EXPEDITIONS
2625 Garnet Avenue
San Diego, CA 92109
800-843-6967 or 619-581-3311
Baja, Costa Rica

COASTAL KAYAKING TOURS INC.
P. O. Box 405
Bar Harbor, ME 04609
800-526-8615 or 207-288-9605
Maine Island Trail, U.S. and British Virgin Islands during winter months

EXPLORERS AT SEA
P. O. Box 51-0
Stonington, ME 04681
207-367-2356
Maine's Penobscot Bay

GEOFF EVANS' KAYAKING CENTRE
Box 97, Cultus Lake
BC, Canada V0X 1H0
604-858-6775
Canadian northwest

NATIONAL OUTDOOR LEADERSHIP SCHOOL (NOLS)
P. O. Box AA
Lander, WY 82520
307-332-6973
Mexico, Baja

NORTHERN LIGHTS EXPEDITIONS
5220 NE 180th
Seattle, WA 98155
206-483-1554
Washington and British Columbia coasts

SEA TREK OCEAN KAYAKING CENTER
85 Liberty Ship Way, Suite 110
Sausalito, CA 94945
415-332-4457
Northern California coast

SOUTHWIND SPORTS RESOURCES
1088 Irvine Boulevard, Suite 212
Tustin, CA 92680
714-730-4820
Channel Islands National Park, Lake Mead

SPIRIT WALKER EXPEDITIONS
P. O. Box 240
Gustavus, AK 99826
907-697-2266
Southeast Alaska coast

TOFINO EXPEDITIONS
#114-1837 West 4th Avenue
Vancouver,
British Columbia
Canada V6J 1M4
604-737-2030
Fax: 604-737-7348
Vancouver Island, Baja

In addition, in the West, outfitters should belong to one of these organizations:

IDAHO OUTFITTERS AND GUIDES ASSOCIATION, INC.
PO Box 95
Boise, ID 83701
208-342-1438

MONTANA OUTFITTERS AND GUIDES ASSOCIATION
PO Box 1248
Helena, MT 59624
406-449-3578

OREGON GUIDES AND PACKERS, INC.
PO Box 132
Sublimity, OR 93785

MAGAZINES
Kayaking magazines are chock full of techniques, recommendations, and usually ample back sections with advertisements for outfitters, organizations and trips.

American Canoeist
Bimonthly newsletter published by the American Canoe Associa-

tion (see address on page 181 under "Organizations").

American Whitewater
Bimonthly published by the American Whitewater Affiliation (see address on page 181 under "Organizations"). This one's for *serious* kayakers.

Canoe & Kayak
Canoe America Associates
Box 3146
Kirkland, WA 98083
206-827-6363
Formerly *Canoe*, a bimonthly

Canoe and Kayak Racing News
PO Box 3146
Kirkland, WA 98083
The racing scene, all over the world. Bimonthly.

Canoe News
Bimonthly newsletter of the U.S. Canoe Association (see address page 181 under "Organizations").

Currents
Quarterly published by National Organization for River Sports (see address page 181 under "Organizations"). Whitewater sports, river conservation and related policies.

Folding Kayaker
PO Box 0754
Planetarium Station
New York, NY 10024

Paddler
4061 Oceanside Blvd., Suite M
Oceanside, CA 92056
619-633-2293
Formerly *River Runner*, covers whitewater canoeing, rafting and kayaking.

Sea Kayaker
PO Box 17170
Seattle, WA 98107-0870
206-789-6413
"The" magazine on this sport.

THE INTERNET
Kayaking on the 'Net? Give it a try. Remember that things change swiftly on the 'Net, so all information provided below can only be guaranteed at the time of publication.

Here are three Internet mailing lists specifically related to White-water Paddling.

Send mail with the word SUB-SCRIBE in the text body to: *WHITEWATER-REQUEST@ GYNKO.CIRC.UPENN.EDU*

Subscribe to the *WHITWATER@ PEAK.ORG* list by sending mail to: *MAJORDOMO@PEAK.ORG.* Type "SUBSCRIBE WHITE-WATER your-e-mail-address."

The New York City Kayaker list is reached by sending e-mail with the words SUBSCRIBE NYCK-AYAKER to *MAJORDOMO@ WORLD.STD.COM.*

America OnWater is an electronic bulletin board providing access to discussion groups (or "conferences") covering diverse topics such as kayaking ecology, choosing equipment, telecommunications in the wilderness, boat testing and rescue methods. Download navigational charts or list items to buy, sell, or trade. An "Ask the Experts" forum answers questions via e-mail. To register with AOW, call the BBS phone number 619-222-3105 by computer modem. For more information, contact Ed Gillett, Southwest Kayaks, 1310 Rosecrans Street, San Diego, CA 92106. 619-222-3616; Fax 619-222-3671 or e-mail to KayakEd@AOL.

A sea kayaking FAQ (frequently asked questions) is available by FTP from VOLT.IEM.EDU.PL (in the directory /PUB/KAYAK) or, for a World Wide Web version, go to *HTTP://SALK. EDU/~PRESTON/KAYAK/SFAQ/ TOC.HTML.*

Although originally a whitewater forum, the usegroup REC. BOATS.PADDLE has more and more information and discussion about sea kayaking and canoeing.

The California Kayak Friends maintain their monthly newsletter, *KayakYak* on the Web: *http://www.intelenet. com/clubs/ckf/yak.*

Wave-Length Paddling Magazine, a publication about protecting the wilderness and sea kayaking, is also online, at *http://www.inte-lenet.com/clubs/ckf/wavelength..* They also maintain a mailing list at the address: *Wave-Length-Request@bbs.sd68.nanaimo.bc.ca.* Send a message saying "subscribe wave-length."

For those of you considering subscribing to a commercial online provider, *America Online* has two outdoor services: Outdoor Adventure Online and Trailside. Outdoor Adventure is a travel and recreation service listing outfitters, organizations and providers of lodging. It also has an active message board for travelers. The Trailside service has up-to-date information about the television series with station carriage updates, downloadable Trailside photos, outfitter information, program descriptions, online chat room, and bulletin boards where users post messages. Users can ask questions directly to the Trailside crew regarding the series and also purchase any merchandise in our Trailside store. Belonging to AOL is a good way to access other groups. To subscribe, call 800-827-6364, Ext. 10380. The software will be provided to you free.

BOOKS
If you like to read or feel better easing slowly into this new venture, here are some suggestions.

TECHNIQUES OF KAYAK TOURING
The Essential Sea Kayaker: A Complete Course for the Open Water Paddler, David Seidman. 1992. Paper. $12.95. McGraw-Hill. This well-organized manual includes sections on paddling with children and kayaking for the disabled.

Marine Books Sea Kayaking Basics, David Harrison. 1993. $15.00. William Morrow & Company. A primer on equipment and techniques.

Sea Kayaking, Nigel Foster. 1990. $59.00. State Mutual Book. A manual of beginner to intermediate technique, particularly strong on ocean morphology, navigation, and surf launching and landing.

TECHNIQUES OF WHITEWATER TOURING
The Bombproof Roll & Beyond, Paul Dutky. 1993. Paper. $14.95. Menasha Ridge Press. The Eskimo roll and related techniques.

Kayak: The Animated Manual of Intermediate & Advanced Whitewater Technique, William Nealy. 1986. Paper. $12.95. Menasha Ridge Press. A comic-strip-format volume from kayaking's iconoclast. In between the gags and ribaldry, this is one of the better manuals of intermediate and advanced whitewater boating, with valuable information on signaling, rescues, and techniques for running major hydraulics.

The Kayaking Book, Eric Evans and Jay Evans. 1988. $12.95. Stephen Greene Press. For both beginners and advanced.

Performance Kayaking, Stephen B. U'ren. 1990. Paper. $15.95. Stackpole Books. U.S. National Whitewater teams demonstrate techniques.

White Water Kayaking, Ray Rowe. 1989. Paper. $15.95. Stackpole Books. Covers the basics of whitewater kayaking, but also includes extensive treatment of advanced big-water activities and techniques.

OTHER FORMS OF KAYAKING
Complete Folding Kayaker, Ralph A. Diaz. 1994. Paperback. $14.95. McGraw-Hill. Everything about break-downable kayaks, including a consumer's guide organized by quality, handling, and ease of assembly.

The Squirt Book: The Manual of Squirt Kayaking Technique, James E. Snyder, illustrated by William Nealy. 1987. Paper. $9.95. Menasha Ridge Press. Designed for the boater with a solid grounding in whitewater, this book devotes a detailed chapter to each of over twenty squirt-boating moves and maneuvers.

The Ultimate Run: Canoe Slalom at the Highest Levels, William Endicott. 1983. (out of print) Endicott.

NARRATIVES
Baidarka: The Kayak, George Dyson. 1986. Paper. $24.95. Alaska Northwest Books. The gorgeous photos and the text in this book present a definitive history of the Aleut kayak.

The Hidden Coast: Kayak Explorations from Alaska to Mexico, Joel W. Rogers. 1991. Paper. $19.95. Alaska Northwest Books.

The Happy Isles of Oceania: Paddling the Pacific, Paul Theroux. 1993. Paper. $12.95. Fawcett Book Group.

Kayaks to Hell, William Nealy. 1982. Paper. $5.95. Menasha Ridge Press. Noted for its photograph of the author demonstrating an ender in a hot tub.

Water's Edge: Women Who Push the Limits in Rowing, Kayaking & Canoeing, Linda Lewis. 1992. Paper. $14.95. Seal Press-Feminist.

Whitewater Tales of Terror, William Nealy. 1983. Paper. $6.95. Menasha Ridge Press. Irreverent, vulgar and hilarious comic book of kayakers *in extremis*.

SAFETY AND RESCUE
Advanced First Aid Afloat, Peter F. Eastman. 4th ed. 1994. Paper. $14.95. Cornell Maritime Press.

How to Survive on Land & Sea, Frank C. Craighead, Jr. & John J. Craighead. 4th ed. 1984. $17.95. Naval Institute Press. A comprehensive manual of survival techniques, equipment and strategies for a broad spectrum of emergency situations.

Hypothermia, Frostbite & Other Cold Injuries: Prevention, Recognition, Pre Hospital Treatment, James A. Wilkerson, et. al., editors. 1986. Paper. $11.95. The Mountaineers.

Medicine for the Backcountry, Buck Tilton. 1994. $12.99. ICS Books. Managing acute injuries in isolated places.

River Rescue, Les Bechdel & Slim Ray. 1989. Paper. $12.95. Appalachian Mountain Club. How to avoid river accidents and how to handle them.

BUILDING BOATS
Boatbuilder's Manual, Charles Walbridge. 1987. Paper. $9.95. Menasha Ridge Press.

Canoes & Kayaks for the Backyard Builder, Skip Snaith. 1988. $19.95. International Marine Publishing.

Wood & Canvas Kayak Building, George Putz. 1990. $17.95. International Marine Publishing.

THE DISABLED BOATER
Canoeing & Kayaking for Persons with Physical Disabilities: Instruction Manual, Anne W. Webre & Janet A. Zeller. 1990. $14.95. American Canoe Association.

International Directory of Recreation-Oriented Assistive Device Sources, Abby K. Lazerow. (out of print) 1986. Lifeboat Press.

An Introduction to Kayaking: for Persons with Disabilities, John H. Galland. (out of print) 1981. Vinland National Center.

KNOTS

The Ashley Book of Knots, Clifford W. Ashley 1993. $50.00. Doubleday & Company.

The Klutz Book of Knots, John Cassidy. 1985. Paper. $9.95. Klutz Press.

Morrow's Guide to Knots: For Sailing Fishing, Camping & Climbing, Maria Bigon & Guido Regazzoni, 1982. Paper. $12.95. William Morrow & Company.

NAVIGATION AND WEATHER

The Boater's Weather Guide, Margaret Williams. 1991. Paper. $6.95. Cornell Maritime Press.

Fundamentals of Kayak Navigation, David Burch. 1993. Paper. $14.95. Globe Pequot Press.

Navigation Rules, International, Inland. rev. ed. 1990. Paper. $6.00. United States Government Printing Office.

FOOD

Cooking on the Go, Janet Groene. 1987. Paper. $10.95. Hearst Books.

Kayak Cookery: A Handbook of Provisions and Recipes, Linda Daniel. (out of print) 1988. Globe Pequot Press.

River Runner's Special: Favorite Recipes of the NOC Restaurant. 1985. $7.00 Nantahala Outdoor Center.

AND MORE...

The Active Travel Resource Guide, Dan Browdy, ed. $19.95. Ultimate Ventures The latest edition lists 85 organizations and the tours they offer, dates, prices, and all.

At the Sea's Edge: An Introduction to Coastal Oceanography for the Amateur Naturalist, William Fox. 1983. Prentice Hall.

The Complete Wilderness Paddler, James W. Davidson & John Rugge. 1982. Paper. $12.00. Random House.

DESTINATION GUIDES

There are excellent navigation guides for almost all of the states, in addition to these more general guides.

The Whitewater Sourcebook, Richard Penny. 1990. Paper. $19.95. Menasha Ridge Press. This large manual provides detailed information on hundreds of rivers in 34 states, as well as sources for maps; lists of organizations, schools, kayaking events; and a priceless list of whitewater guidebooks for each state.

Appalachian Whitewater, Vols 1 and II, 1986/87. $13.95/14.95. Menasha Ridge Press.

New England Whitewater River Guide, Ray Gabler. 1981. $14.95. Appalachian Mountain Club. Maps and descriptions of 62 whitewater runs.

Sea Kayaking Along the Mid-Atlantic Coast: Coastal Paddling Adventures from New York, Tamsin Venn. 1994. $14.95. Appalachian Mountain Club.

Sea Kayaking Along the New England Coast. Tamsin Venn. 1990. $14.95. Appalachian Mountain Club.

Western Whitewater from the Rockies to the Pacific: A River Guide for Raft, Kayak, & Canoe, Jim Cassady, et. al. 1994. $34.95. North Forks Press. The definitive guide to kayaking in a huge chunk of the States.

Whitewater Quietwater, Bob Palzer & Jody Palzer. 1983. $12.95. Menasha Ridge Press. Guides to 750 miles of rivers in the Great Lakes region.

VIDEOS

Our own Trailside series of videos which aired on Public Television is one of the greatest inspirations we can offer to the novice kayaker.

Glacier Kayaking in Alaska. Paddle in a foldable kayak and camp with Doug Fesler in Prince William Sound. 40 minutes, $19.98, to order call 1-800-TRAILSIDE (1-800-872-4573).

Sea Kayaking in Baja. Learn how to load a kayak, plan a trip, launch into surf and keep your cool among the sea lions. 40 minutes, $19.98, to order call 1-800-TRAILSIDE (1-800-872-4573).

Sea Kayaking the Maine Island Trail. Sharpen your navigational skills paddling this watery version of the Appalachian Trail on the beautiful, rugged Maine coast. 40 minutes, $19.95, to order call 1-800-TRAILSIDE (1-800-872-4573).

Whitewater Kayaking in Oregon. Hayden Glatte and Brian Tooley teach you how to whitewater in Class 4 rapids on the Rogue River. 40 minutes, $19.98, to order call 1-800-TRAILSIDE (1-800-872-4573).

OTHER INSTRUCTIONAL VIDEOS

To order, try the mail-order sources listed in the next section.

Grace Under Pressure: Learning the Kayak Roll. A comprehensive learning video with Nantahala's instructors. 45 minutes, $30.00.

Heads Up! River Rescue for River Runners. Produced in association with the U.S. Coast Guard and the American Canoe Association, $40.00.

Kayak Handling. Basic strokes with Richard Fox. 43 minutes, $30.00.

Kayaker's Edge. Beginning through advanced strokes. 58 minutes, $31.95.

Kayaking Basics: Paddling with Olympic Champion Greg Barton, $26.99.

KAYAK ACTION

A Token of My Extreme. Inflatable kayaks pushed to the limits by Jeff Snyder. 36 minutes, $29.95.

Plunge. Vertical kayaking in the South, plus the Ocoee Rodeo. 45 minutes, $26.95.

Southern Fried Creekin. Wild creek boating. 45 minutes, $26.95.

Slammin' Salmon/Bloopers 2. Rafters and kayakers at their wildest. 40 minutes, $21.95.

Take the Wild Ride. Instructional shots at the Whitewater World Championships Rodeo. 52 minutes, $29.95.

Vertical Addiction. Featuring Wayne Gentry. 45 minutes, $26.95.

MAIL-ORDER SOURCES OF BOOKS AND GEAR

If one doesn't have what you're looking for, another is sure to. Here are just a few mail-order suppliers.

ADVENTUROUS TRAVELER BOOKSTORE

PO Box 577
Hinesburg, VT 05461
800-282-3963 or 802-482-3330
Fax: 800-282-3963,
802-482-3546.
E-mail: books@atbook.com; on the World Wide Web —
http://www.gorp.com/atbook.htm
— search their full selection of 3,000 titles by keyword. Largest supplier of worldwide adventure travel books and maps.

BACKCOUNTRY BOOKSTORE

PO Box 6235
Lynnwood, WA 90836-0235
206-290-7652
Books and videos on all outdoor activities, as well as knowledgeable staff.

BOUNDARY WATERS CATALOG, PIRAGIS NORTHWOODS COMPANY

105R North Central Ave.
Ely, MN 55731
800-223-6565
Full line of gear.

L. L. BEAN

Casco St.
Freeport, ME 04033
800-221-4221.

NANTAHALA OUTDOOR CENTER (NOC)

13077 Hwy 19 West
Bryson City, NC 28713-9114
800-367-3521
Fax: 704-488-8039
Besides a mail order catalog of everything you might want, Nantahala runs custom programs in whitewater instruction and rafting.

PADDLE STUFF

1634 South Nevada St.
Oceanside, CA 92054
800-747-6628
Videos, books, etc.

STOHLQUIST/COLORADO KAYAK SUPPLY

PO Box 3059
Buena Vista, CO 81211.
800-535-3565
Fax: 719-395-2421
See full line of kayaks and accessories, including books and videos.

VIDEO ACTION SPORTS

200 Suburban Road, Suite E
San Luis Obispo, CA 93401
800-727-6689 or 805-543-4812.

KAYAK MANUFACTURERS

A full list of manufacturers is carried in the gear guides published in several of the leading paddling magazines each year. These are just a portion of those out there:

ACE & MI DESIGNS

USA: Impex International
1107 Station Rd.
Bellport, NY 11713
516-286-1988
CANADA: Scott Canoe
Box 1599
New Liskeard
Ontario, Canada P0J 1P0
705-647-6548
touring

AQUATERRA

PO Box 8002
Easley, SC 29641
803-859-7518
touring

B & A DISTRIBUTING CO.

201 S.E. Oak St.
Portland, OR 97214-1079
503-230-0482
inflatable

BETSIE BAY KAYAK

PO Box 1706
Frankfort, MI 49635
616-352-7774
touring

CHESAPEAKE LIGHT CRAFT

34 S. Pershing Dr.
Arlington, VA 22204
703-271-8787
touring

CURRENT DESIGNS

10124-G McDonald Park Rd.
Sidney, British Columbia
Canada V8L 3X9
604-655-1822
touring

DAGGER CANOE COMPANY

PO Box 1500
Harriman, TN 37748
615-882-0404
whitewater, touring

DESTINY KAYAK CO.

1604 Center St.
Tacoma, WA 98405
206-572-5742
touring

EASY RIDER CANOE & KAYAK

PO Box 88108
Seattle, WA 98138
206-228-3633
whitewater, touring

EDDYLINE KAYAKS
1344 Ashten Rd.
Burlington, WA 98233
206-757-2300
touring

ENGLEHART PRODUCTS
1808 Owen Road
Middlefield, OH 44062
216-548-2096
whitewater

EURO KAYAKS/L'EAU VIE
PO Box 65
Twin Lakes, CO 81251
719-486-1114
whitewater, touring, sit-on-top

FEATHERCRAFT PRODUCTS, LTD.
#4-1244 Cartwright St.
Vancouver, British Columbia,
Canada V6H 3R8
604-681-8437
touring, folding

GREAT RIVER OUTFITTERS
3721 Shallow Brook
Bloomfield Hills, MI 48302
313-644-6909
touring

HYSIDE INFLATABLES
PO Box Z
Kernville, CA 93238
619-376-3723
inflatable

HYDRA KAYAKS
5061 South National Drive
Knoxville, TN 37914
800-537-8888
whitewater, touring, sit-on-top

KIWI KAYAKS
PO Box 1140
Windsor, CA 95492
707-433-9544
800-545-2925
whitewater, touring, sit-on-top

KLEPPER AMERICA
168 Kindermack Rd.
Park Ridge, NJ 07656
201-476-0700
touring

MARINER KAYAKS
2134 Westlake Ave. N.
Seattle, WA 98109
206-284-8404
touring

NECKY KAYAKS
1100 Riverside Rd.
Abbotsford, British Columbia
Canada V2S 4N2
604-850-1206
touring, sit-on-top

MOMENTUM
see B & A Distributing Co.

NEW WAVE KAYAK PRODUCTS
2535 Roundtop Road
Middletown, PA 17057
717-944-6320
whitewater

**NEW YORK KAYAK CO./
NAUTIRAID**
PO Box 2011
Old Chelsea Station
New York, NY 11011
212-613-9080
touring

NORTHSHORE DESIGNS
see ACE & MI Designs
touring

NORTHWEST KAYAKS
15145 NE 90th St.
Redmond, WA 98052-3560
206-869-1107
800-648-8908
touring

OCEAN KAYAK, INC.
2460 Grandview Rd.
Ferndale, WA 98248
800-8KAYAKS
360-366-4003
sit-on-top

OLD TOWN CANOE CO.
58 Middle St.
Old Town, ME 04468
207-827-5513
sit-on-top

P & H DESIGN
see ACE & MI Designs
touring

PACIFIC CANOE BASE
562 David St.
Victoria, British Columbia
Canada V8T 2C8
604-382-1243
touring

PACIFIC WATER SPORTS
16055 Pacific Highway South
Seattle, WA 98188
206-246-9385
touring

PERCEPTION, INC.
PO Box 8002
Easley, SC 29641
803-859-7518
whitewater

PHOENIX PRODUCTS
PO Box 109
207 N. Broadway
Berea, KY 40403
800-354-0190
whitewater, touring

PRIJON/WILDWASSER SPORT
PO Box 4617
Boulder, CO 80306
303-444-2336
whitewater, touring, sit-on-top

PYRANHA KAYAKS
see ACE & MI Designs
whitewater, touring

RIKEN
see B & A Distributing Co.

SEDA PRODUCTS
926 Coolidge Ave.
National City, CA 91950
619-336-2444
whitewater, touring

**SOUTHERN EXPOSURE
SEA KAYAKS**
18487 U.S. Hwy. 1
Tequesta, FL 33469
407-575-4530
touring

SUPERIOR KAYAKS, INC.
108 Menasha Ave.
PO Box 355
Whitelaw, WI 54247-0355
414-732-3784
touring

TSUNAMI PRODUCTS
13732 Bear Mountain Rd.
Redding, CA 96003
916-275-4313
sit-on-top

THE UPSTREAM EDGE
699 Speedvale Avenue West
Guelph, Ontario
Canada N1K 1E6
519-824-1415
whitewater

VALLEY CANOE PRODUCTS
see Great River Outfitters

VALHALLA SURF SKI PRODUCTS
4724 Renex Place
San Diego, CA 92117
619-569-1395
sit-on-top

**VENTURESPORTS SURF
SKI PRODUCTS**
PO Box 610145
N. Miami, FL 33261
407-395-1376
sit-on-top

WALDEN PADDLERS
PO Box 647
Concord, MA 01742
508-371-3000
touring

WAVE SPORTS, INC.
PO Box 5207
Steamboat Springs, CO 80477
303-736-0080
whitewater

WE-NO-NAH CANOE, INC.
PO Box 247
Winona, MN 55987
507-454-5430
touring

WEST SIDE BOAT SHOP
7661 Tonawanda Creek Road
Lockport, NY 14094
716-434-5755
touring

WILDERNESS SYSTEMS
241 Woodbine St.
High Point, NC 27260
910-883-7410
touring

WOODSTRIP WATERCRAFT
1818 Swamp Pike
Gilbertsville, PA 19525
215-326-9282
touring

P H O T O
C R E D I T S

DUGALD BREMNER: 13, 14, 16, 17, 18, 41, 43, 44, 46, 52, 58, 82, 83, 125, 138, 152

SKIP BROWN: 60, 61, 93, 137, 149, 161, 164, 168

JOHN GOODMAN: 11, 19, 20-21 (BOTH), 22-23 (BOTH), 29 (ALL), 30, 31, 32 (ALL), 34 (ALL), 35, 36 (BOTH), 37, 65, 71 (BOTH), 73, 74, 75, 79, 95, 105, 109, 110, 111, 115, 151, 163, 169

ROB LESSER: 129, 143, 145, 165, 166, 177

CHRIS NOBLE: 49, 118

KEVIN O'BRIEN: 48, 122, 141

SLIM RAY: 40, 51, 57, 64, 117, 121, 127, 128 (BOTH), 134, 135, 150, 157

JOEL W. RODGERS: 12, 15, 38, 42 (BOTH), 50, 53 (ALL), 66, 68 (BOTH), 70, 77, 81, 84, 89, 91, 96, 97, 100, 103, 107, 112, 113, 170, 175, 180

SCOTT SPIKER: 62, 72, 120, 133

INDEX